Southern Keto Cookbook

100 Classic Traditional High-Fat, Low-Carb Recipes

Diane Brown

ISBN-13: 979- 8649273848

DEDICATION

To all who desire to live life to the fullest!

TABLE OF CONTENT

INTRODUCTION

The Southern Cuisine is all about tradition; a tradition of people, family and friends. A tradition built on the strong beliefs of love, perseverance and togetherness. A tradition that has defined the American South, and this tradition is one that should be preserved for generations to come and be handed down to our children's children like it was in the time of our grandparents.

Most of the Southern Cuisine elements were gotten from Europe, West Country of England, Scotland, West Africa and the Southeast American Indian tribes. And these has defined the way the people of the South eat.

It was on foundations, such as these that the taste buds of my siblings and I were built on. The fondness of a full breakfast of pan-fried chicken, greens & peas, mashed potatoes, cornbread sweet tea, and cobbler for dessert. And over the years I have had to rediscover the secret that made the Cuisine stand out and find a way for it to work for my health.

I have discovered the effectiveness of the Ketogenic diet within the Southern meals, that has helped me and my family to live healthy for years while maintaining our Southern heritage.

In this cookbook, you will discover the secret high fat and low carb Southern recipes, and begin to enjoy from the well of health benefits existent on the Ketogenic diet while also satisfying your cravings for classic Southern meal.

Whether you are new to the Southern way of eating or a pro in Southern Cuisine, this cookbook is a must have on the quest to tasty and healthy traditional Southern meals.

THE SOUTHERN CUISINE

The Southern food has a sort of uniqueness to itself, an honor used only in the identification for the cuisine of France, Mexico, Italy & China. But over the years, the Southern Cuisine has proven worthy to be able to stand among the greats.

A cuisine as varied and diverse and equally as interesting as its history, the Southern Cuisine has become one of America's favorite over the years.

The tradition Southern way of cooking, also referred to the country cooking, is known for been high in fat, sugar & calories, relying majorly on pork, corn & rice, chicken, vegetables and seafood as the main ingredients.

History of the Southern Cuisine

A mixture of different cultural influences from around the world has helped shape the Southern food into what it is today.

When the first Europeans migrated to North America, they settled down in the Southern region of America and came with a variety of their own seeds and vegetables and with time, the South Americans started to adopt the immigrant's food into their own diets.

Similarly, the Scottish and West Africans brought their own vegetables, grains and ingredients such as; yams, eggplant, okra, black-eyed peas, watermelon with their unique style of cooking and all these was soon adopted into the Southern Cuisine.

Over the years, a blend of homegrown greens of kale, collards, turnips and that of the foreign import has shaped the foundation of the Southern Cuisine, with an ever evolving diversity based on the change in demographics.

Difference between Soul Food and Southern Food

It's very difficult to differentiate Soul food from Southern food. The two are basically the same food and just depends on whether you prefer to call it soul food or southern food, although, while all Soul food are basically Southern food, not all Southern food is considered a Soul food.

People have defined Soul food as a way of cooking that was derived from the West African way of cooking, a basic cooking method, that originated in the rural part of the South and has evolved over the years. The major difference between the two, is the history and culture behind each one and sometimes; the seasoning used in preparation.

Soul food holds a special meaning to many African Americans, getting its moniker in the 1960s, as part of the Civil Rights era's Black Pride movement, celebrating the pride, ingenuity and perseverance involved in overcoming affliction.

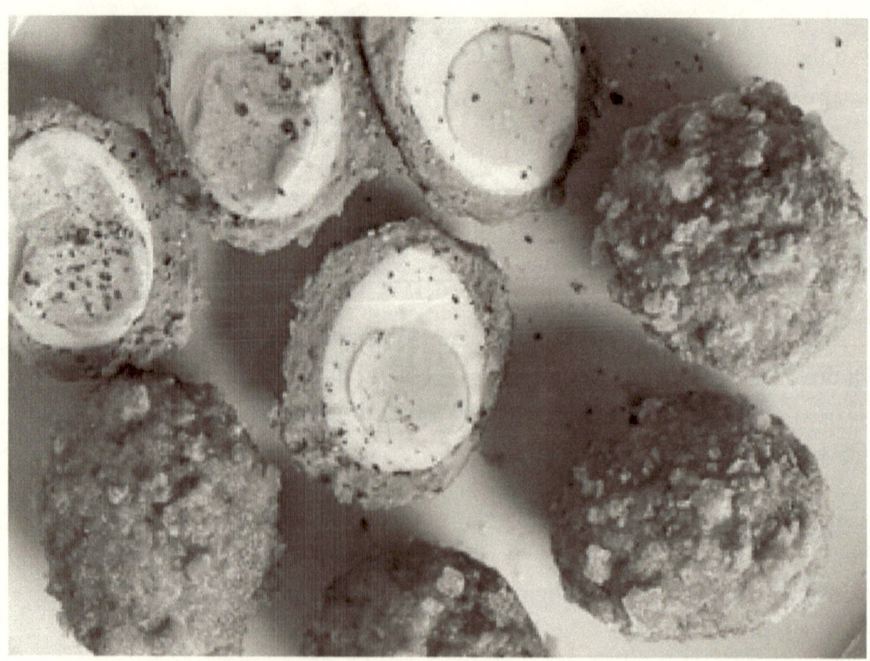

THE KETO BASICS

Ketogenic diet is a low carbohydrate, high fat, moderate protein diet, that allows the body system to produces ketones in the liver, instead of glucose which is the main source of energy in the body. It is also referred to as a low carb diet, keto diet or low carb high fat (LCHF) diet etc.

The major goal of a ketogenic diet is to burn the body fat as a source of energy thereby leading it a healthy and effective weight loss.

Becoming Keto Adapted

Being keto adapted is a state in which the body starts to burn fats instead of carbohydrate and produces ketones for energy. There are two main ways by which the body can become keto-adapted;

- Reduce excessive intake of carbohydrate food.

- Eat more of fats.

Ketosis

When you consume foods that are high in carbohydrate, the body system produces glucose and insulin. Glucose is the simplest molecule in the body, that can be reproduced to be used as energy, so it is usually chosen over every other source of energy. While the insulin serves as the catalyst, that takes the glucose around the body via the bloodstream.

Since carbohydrate is the source of the primary form of energy in the body, the fats consumed are not been used, instead they are stored in the body. But when you reduce the intake of carbohydrate food, the body is induced into a ketosis state.

Ketosis is a natural process the body embarks on when the food intake is low, in other to survive. While in this state, the body system produces ketones; ketones are formed from the breakdown of fats in the liver

What are ketones?

When you replace the excess intake of carbohydrate with that of fats, the body begins to burn ketones as the primary source of energy. Optimal levels of ketone offer many health, physical, weight loss and metal performance benefits.

Types of Ketone Bodies

There are three known ketone bodies which are water-soluble molecules that are created by the liver from fatty acids.

- Acetoacetate

- Beta-Hydroxybutyrate

- Acetone

These ketone bodies are picked up by the extra-hepatic tissues and processed into Acetyl-CoA which is then transported into the citric acid cycle and is oxidized in the mitochondria for energy.

Types of Ketogenic Diet

There are four types of ketogenic diet, each depending on the dieter and expected result from the diet. Below are the three versions of ketogenic diet available.

Standard Ketogenic Diet; this is the regular and most popular with low carbohydrate, high fat and moderate protein. It usually contains 75% fat, 20% protein and 5% carbs

High-Protein Ketogenic Diet; this is very similar to the standard ketogenic diet, but allows more protein with the ratio often at 60% fat, 35% protein and 5% carbs.

Cyclical Ketogenic Diet; this type of ketogenic diet allows for a period of higher intake of carbohydrate. For instance, 5 days of the standard ketogenic diet with 2 days of high carbohydrate intake.

Targeted Ketogenic Diet; this type is usually employed by athletes and body builders; it allows them to add extra carbohydrates around their work out routines

Although, only the standard and high-protein ketogenic diets have been extensively studied extensively.

Benefits of the Ketogenic Diet

The ketogenic diet offers its dieters health benefits, from rapid weight loss, improved mental alertness to effective heart disease management.

Below is a list of health benefits you stand to enjoy from the ketogenic diet;

- Lose of body fat and weight management
- Increased levels of good cholesterol
- A reduced insulin resistance and blood sugar level
- Controlled appetite and longer satiation
- Increased body energy and brain power
- Reductions in triglyceride levels and blood pressure

Keto Foods & Which Ones You Should Avoid

When starting a ketogenic diet, you have to plan ahead of time. Your plan majorly depends on how soon you want to get into the ketogenic form. The more you restrain yourself from taking high carbohydrate foods (less than 15g per day), the sooner you start to experience ketosis.

Your nutrient intake should be around 70% of fats, 25% of protein, and 5% of carbohydrate.

What to Eat

- **Fats:** Coconut oil, saturated fats, high-fat salad dressing and so on.
- **Poultry:** Eggs, fish, beef, lamb, meats and so on.
- **Sweeteners:** Stevia, erythritol, monk fruit and other low carb sweeteners.
- **Leafy Greens:** Kale, spinach and so on.
- **High fat dairy:** Butter, hard cheeses, high fat cream and so on.
- **Nuts and seeds:** Walnuts, macadamias, sunflower seeds and so on.
- **Top ground veggies:** Broccoli, cauliflower and so on.
- **Avocado and berries:** Blackberries, raspberries and other little glycemic berries.

What Not to Eat

- **Fruit:** Apples, oranges, bananas and so on.
- **Sugar:** Agave and so on.
- **Drinks:** Soda and beer.
- **Tubers:** Yams, potatoes and so on.
- **Grains:** Corn, rice, wheat, cereal and so on.

BREAKFAST, BRUNCH & BREAD RECIPES

Coconut Flour & Cream Pancakes

Preparation Time: 15 minutes

Cook Time: 15 minutes

Servings: 3

Ingredients

1/4 teaspoon Himalayan salt

1/2 teaspoon cinnamon

1/2 cup coconut cream

1/2 cup coconut flour

1/2 teaspoon baking soda

1/2 cup unsweetened almond milk

1 teaspoon vanilla

2 tablespoons melted coconut oil

4 large eggs

ghee, to cook

Instructions

1. Using a high speed blender, add in all the ingredients (except the ghee) and blend until fully combined.

2. Using a medium skillet, add in the ghee and heat over medium heat then pour in 1/2 cup of the batter mixture.

3. Cook the dough until golden on one side then flip over and cook the other side until also golden then set aside.

4. Cook the remaining batter until golden then serve and enjoy with any topping of your choice.

Nutrition Information

Calories: 244kcal | Fat: 23g | Carbohydrates: 4.9g | Protein: 5.5g

Cinnamon Toast Crunch

Preparation Time: 20 minutes

Cook Time: 15 minutes

Servings: 10

Ingredients

1/4 teaspoon kosher salt

1/2 teaspoon xanthan gum

1/2 teaspoon baking soda

1 large egg

2 teaspoons ground cinnamon

80g butter

96g erythritol

192g almond flour

for the topping

2 tablespoons swerve

2 teaspoons ground cinnamon sugar

28g melted butter

Instructions

1. Using a medium sized mixing bowl, add in the salt, baking soda, cinnamon, xanthum gum, almond flour and mix together until combined.

2. Using an electric mixer, whisk the butter for 2-3 minutes then pour in the sweetener and continue to beat until fluffy and light.

3. Add the egg into the mixture and mix until combined then pour in half of the flour mixture, combine and add in the remaining half and mix.

4. Tightly wrap the dough with a cling film then refrigerate for an hour after which you heat the oven up to 350°F.

5. Roll the refrigerated dough out between two parchment paper until thin and vertically slice then crosswise into squares.

6. Transfer the parchment paper onto a baking sheet then refrigerate for 15 minutes then bake in the oven until fully golden for 10-12 minutes.

7. Coat the crunches with the melted butter and top with cinnamon sugar then allow to cool off.

8. Serve and enjoy as desired.

Nutrition Information

Calories: 172kcal | Fat: 16g | Carbohydrates: 4g | Protein: 4g

Cinnamon Chocolate Donuts

Preparation Time: 20 minutes

Cook Time: 10 minutes

Servings: 5

Ingredients

for the donuts

1/2 cup green banana flour

1 teaspoon baking powder

1 tablespoon melted butter

1 tablespoon powdered cacao

1 teaspoon apple cider vinegar

2 large eggs

2 teaspoons vanilla extract

3 teaspoons cinnamon sugar

3 tablespoons granulated sweetener

4 tablespoons coconut milk

a pinch of salt

coconut oil for greasing

for the topping

1/4 avocado

1 1/2 teaspoons powdered cacao

4 tablespoons coconut cream

stevia drops, to taste,

vanilla extract, to taste

shredded coconut, if desired

Instructions

1. Heat the oven up to 350°F then grease a baking pan with the coconut oil and set aside.

2. Using a large mixing bowl, add in all the ingredients and incorporate together until combined.

3. Evenly divide the batter mix into donut molds until 3/4 full and place into the greased pan.

4. Bake the donuts until cooked through for 8-10 minutes then set out to cool off.

5. Combine all the topping ingredients together (except the shredded coconut) until smooth and blended.

6. Top the donuts with the topping mix and enjoy, garnished with the shredded coconut.

Nutrition Information

Calories: 112kcal | Fat: 6.6g | Carbohydrates: 13.6g | Protein: 3g

Eggs & Sausage Muffin

Preparation Time: 10 minutes

Cook Time: 10 minutes

Servings: 1

Ingredients

1/4 cup water

1/4-pound pork breakfast sausage

2 large eggs

2 tablespoons guacamole, if desired

2 tablespoons divided ghee, with extra for greasing

kosher salt & black pepper, to taste

Instructions

1. Grease two biscuit cutters with the extra ghee and fill one with the pork sausage and press down until a uniform shape is reached.

2. Place a medium skillet over medium heat and heat up a tablespoon of ghee then add in the shaped sausage patty when hot and fry until fully cooked for 3 minutes per side.

3. Break the eggs into two small bowls then heat the remaining ghee over medium high heat then pour egg mixtures into the two biscuit cutters and place the cutter into the pan.

4. Season the eggs in the cutters with the salt and pepper then add in 1/4 cup water into the skillet, then cover, and cook on low heat until cooked through for 3 minutes.

5. Transfer the eggs onto a kitchen towel lined plate then place the sausage patty on one of the eggs and top with the other egg.

6. Serve, topped with guacamole and enjoy.

Nutrition Information

Calories: 783kcal | Fat: 73g | Carbohydrates: 3g | Protein: 29g

Ketogenic Cinnamon Rolls

Preparation Time: 12 minutes

Cook Time: 30 minutes

Servings: 12

Ingredients

for the cinnamon roll

1 tablespoon apple cider vinegar

1 batch of chilled keto caramel sauce

1 1/2 teaspoons baking powder

2 tablespoons ghee

2 cups macadamia nuts

2 teaspoons vanilla extract

2 tablespoons ground psyllium husks

3 teaspoons Ceylon cinnamon

3 tablespoons sweetened erythritol

4 large eggs

8 tablespoons coconut flour

a pinch of salt

for the glaze

2 teaspoons erythritol

2 tablespoon melted ghee

4 tablespoons coconut cream

Instructions

1. Using a high speed blender, add in the macadamia nuts and grind until smooth with a nice texture.

2. Combine all the cinnamon roll ingredients (except the caramel sauce) together with the grinded nuts then place in the refrigerator for an hour.

3. Heat the oven up to 350°F then prepare a baking sheet with parchment paper then roll out the dough onto the pan, and mold into a big rectangle.

4. Top the rolled dough with the caramel sauce the spread out using the back of a spoon then roll the dough into a log and seal.

5. Slice the log into 12 rolls then arrange on the baking sheet and bake for 25-30 minutes.

6. In the meantime, blend all the ingredients together until combined.

7. Serve the cinnamon rolls and enjoy, topped with the glaze.

Nutrition Information

Calories: 477kcal | Fat: 45.6g | Carbohydrates: 17.1g | Protein: 5.6g

Chocolate Butter Crepes

Preparation Time: 5 minutes

Cook Time: 20 minutes

Servings: 8

Ingredients

for the crepes

1/4 teaspoon sea salt

1/2 cup coconut milk

1/2 teaspoon vanilla extract

3 tablespoons coconut flour

3 teaspoons powdered arrowroot

4 tablespoons melted coconut oil

6 large eggs

ghee, to grease

for the chocolate butter spread

1 teaspoon powdered cacao

4 tablespoons almond butter, unsweetened & unsalted

6 tablespoon coconut milk

a pinch of sea salt

Instructions

1. Whisk all the crepes ingredients together until smooth, mixed and with no lumps then allow to set for 5 minutes.

2. Add a teaspoon ghee into a skillet and place over medium heat then reduce to a medium low heat once the ghee is heated.

3. Stir the batter together again, then pour 1/4 cup of the batter into skillet, swirl around then cook until the edges begin to crisp for a minute.

4. Flip the batter over and cook the other side until crisp for 30 seconds then set aside to cool and repeat the same process with the remaining batter.

5. Combine all the butter spread ingredients together until smooth and creamy.

6. Enjoy the crepes, served with the butter spread.

Nutrition Information

Calories: 220kcal | Fat: 19.7g | Carbohydrates: 5.1g | Protein: 6.7g

Simple Coconut French Toast

Preparation Time: 15 minutes

Cook Time: 5 minutes

Servings: 3

Ingredients

1/3 cup coconut yogurt

1 tablespoon butter

1 teaspoon vanilla extract

1 coconut flour bread loaf

2 teaspoons of stevia

cacao nibs, if desired

shredded coconut, if desired

Instructions

1. Slice the bread loaf into 3 pieces then vertically half each.

2. Using a medium fry pan, add in the butter, heat over medium heat and swirl the pan to coat.

3. Once the butter is heated, add in 2 pieces of bread and toast until golden on each side.

4. In the meantime add the vanilla, sweetener and coconut yogurt into a mixing bowl and beat with an electric mixer until thicken.

5. Divide the toasted bread between 3 plates and top each with the vanilla mix, cocoa nibs, shredded coconut and enjoy.

Nutrition Information

Calories: 683kcal | Fat: 58g | Carbohydrates: 17g | Protein: 27.9g

Simple Collagen Bread

Preparation Time: 10 minutes

Cook Time: 40 minutes

Servings: 12

Ingredients

1/2 cup collagen protein

1 teaspoon xanthan gum

1 teaspoon baking powder

1 tablespoon coconut oil

5 separated eggs

6 tablespoons almond flour

salt, to taste

Instructions

1. Heat the oven up to 325°F then generously grease a loaf pan with the cooking oil spray.

2. Add the egg whites into a mixing bowl and beat until a stiff peak is formed then set aside.

3. Add the dry ingredients into a separate mixing bowl and whisk together until combined.

4. Whisk the egg yolks and oil together then incorporate with the dry ingredients mixture until thick.

5. Transfer the batter into the greased loaf pan then bake in the oven for 40 minutes.

6. Allow the loaf to cool off then slice into 12, serve and enjoy.

Nutrition Information

Calories: 77kcal | Fat: 5g | Carbohydrates: 1g | Protein: 7g

Zucchini Sauce Butter Cake

Preparation Time: 15 minutes

Cook Time: 55 minutes

Servings: 10

Ingredients

1/4 cup shredded parmesan cheese

1/2 cup heavy cream

1/2 cup diced onion

1 teaspoon Worcestershire sauce

2 pounds diced zucchini

2 tablespoons bread crumbs

3 large eggs

4 tablespoons melted butter

1 dash hot sauce

salt & pepper, to taste

Instructions

1. Heat the oven up to 350°F then add the diced zucchini and butter into a large saucepan.

2. Cook the zucchini over low heat for 5-7 minutes until tenderized then take off the heat and set aside.

3. Combine the heavy cream and eggs together, beating until incorporated.

4. Add 2 tablespoon parmesan cheese, pepper, salt, hot sauce, Worcestershire sauce, onion and breadcrumbs into the eggs mixture and blend in.

5. Add the prepared zucchini into the bowl and blend together then transfer into a cooking oil greased casserole and top with the remaining cheese.

6. Bake, uncovered for 40 minutes then serve and enjoy.

Nutrition Information

Calories: 136kcal | Fat: 11.2g | Carbohydrates: 5.3g | Protein: 3.9g

Simple Cauliflower Florets Blend

Preparation Time: 5 minutes

Cook Time: 5 minutes

Servings: 5

Ingredients

1/3 cup chicken broth

1 chopped medium cauliflower head

2 tablespoons low fat sour cream

thinly sliced chives

salt & pepper, to taste

Instructions

1. Using a microwave safe bowl, add in the cauliflower florets with 1/4 cup of water and microwave until tenderized for 4 minutes.

2. Allow the cauliflower to cool off then transfer into a high speed blender.

3. Add in the sour cream, chicken broth, pepper, salt and puree until smooth and blended.

4. Serve and enjoy, topped with the chives.

Nutrition Information

Calories: 38kcal | Fat: 0.5g | Carbohydrates: 5.5g | Protein: 3g

Ketchup Meatloaf

Preparation Time: 5 minutes

Cook Time: 1 hour

Servings: 8

Ingredients

1/2 cup ketchup

1/2 teaspoon black pepper

1/2 teaspoon powdered garlic

1 teaspoon salt

1 tablespoon powder onion

1 teaspoon dry ground mustard

1 1/2 tablespoon Worcestershire sauce

2 pounds ground beef

3 large eggs

Instructions

1. Heat the oven up to 350°F then add all the ingredients (except the ketchup) into a large bowl and combine.

2. Form the mixture into a loaf then place inside a baking dish and bake for 45 minutes.

3. Take the loaf out of the oven and top with the ketchup, evenly spreading all over.

4. Return the loaf back into the oven and bake for an extra 15 minutes.

5. Allow the loaf to cool off then slice in, serve and enjoy.

Nutrition Information

Calories: 283kcal | Fat: 19g | Carbohydrates: 2g | Protein: 24g

Bacon Fried Cabbage

Preparation Time: 20 minutes

Cook Time: 40 minutes

Servings: 8

Ingredients

1/2 teaspoon paprika

1 large sweet onion

1 large cabbage head, shredded

4 minced garlic cloves

8 bacon slices

kosher salt & pepper, to taste

Instructions

1. Arrange the bacon slices in a single layer in sauté pan and heat for 5 minutes over medium heat then flip over and heat until browned for another 5 minutes.

2. Take the bacon out pan and set aside then add the onion into the pan and sauté until browned for 10 minutes.

3. Add the garlic into the pan and sauté until fragrant for a minute then stir with the onions.

4. Add the shredded cabbage into pan then season with the pepper, salt, paprika, cover and cook until the cabbage is tenderized for 20-25 minutes.

5. In the meantime, chop the browned bacon then stir back into the pan when the cabbage is tenderized.

6. Serve and enjoy as desired.

Nutrition Information

Calories: 143kcal | Fat: 9g | Carbohydrates: 12g | Protein: 5g

Braised Greens & Bacon Slices

Preparation Time: 5 minutes

Cook Time: 50 minutes

Servings: 3

Ingredients

1/2 pound diced bacon slices

1 tablespoon balsamic vinegar

2 bay leaves

2 cups chicken stock

2 sliced thin shallots

2 chopped large bunches of collard greens

5 minced garlic cloves

sea salt, to taste

Instructions

1. Using a large Dutch oven, add in the bacon slices and cook over medium heat until crispy then spoon out of the oven and allow the fat to drain.

2. Add the shallots and garlic into the oven and cook until browned & fragrant for 10 minutes.

3. Add in the greens, salt, vinegar, chicken stock, bay leaves, chopped bacon and stir together.

4. Cover the oven and cook for 30 minutes, uncover the oven and cook until the liquid is evaporated for another 10 minutes.

5. Serve and enjoy.

Nutrition Information

Calories: 143kcal | Fat: 9g | Carbohydrates: 12g | Protein: 5g

Keto Pasta Dough

Preparation Time: 30 minutes

Cook Time: 5 minutes

Servings: 4

Ingredients

1/4 teaspoon kosher salt

1 slightly beaten large

2 teaspoons xanthan gum

2 tablespoons coconut oil

2 teaspoons apple cider vinegar

4 teaspoons water

4 minced garlic cloves

24g coconut flour

96g almond flour

56g unsalted butter

Instructions

1. Using a food processor, add in the xanthum gum, coconut flour, salt, and almond flour then process until incorporated.

2. Add the cider vinegar into the processor and process then pour in the beaten egg and pulse again to combine.

3. Pour water in bits until the dough is molded into a ball, firm and sticky.

4. Transfer the dough into a cling film, knead then allow to sit in the fridge for 30 minutes.

5. Roll the dough out until thin using a rolling pin then press between two parchment paper.

6. Slice the dough into 2" by 1" rectangles then freeze for 15 minutes.

7. Heat the butter & oil on low heat in a large skillet then sauté the garlic until browned.

8. Add in the chilled dough and baste until tenderized with some color.

9. Serve and enjoy with any topping of your choice.

Nutrition Information

Calories: 176kcal | Fat: 13g | Carbohydrates: 8g | Protein: 7g

Herbal Focaccia

Preparation Time: 10 minutes

Cook Time: 20 minutes

Servings: 8

Ingredients

for the flour

1/4 cup coconut flour

1/2 teaspoon xanthan gum

1/2 teaspoon baking soda

1/2 teaspoon baking powder

1 cup almond flour

1 teaspoon sea salt

1 teaspoon powdered garlic

other ingredients

1 tablespoon juiced lime

2 large eggs

2 teaspoons avocado oil, with extra to drizzle

Instructions

1. Heat the oven up to 350°F then line the baking sheet with a large parchment paper.

2. Combine all the flour ingredients together, ensuring there are no lumps in the mixture.

3. Combine oil, eggs, lime juice and beat together until incorporated.

4. Mix the flour ingredients and oil mix together until well blended into the other.

5. Transfer the batter onto the prepared baking sheet then poke holes into the dough to form the focaccia.

6. Place the sheet in the oven and bake for 10 minutes.

7. Drizzle the bread and bake again until lightly brown for 10 minutes.

8. Serve and enjoy with any garnish of your choice.

Nutrition Information

Calories: 166kcal | Fat: 13g | Carbohydrates: 7g | Protein: 7g

Crispy Beans, Bacons & Herbs

Preparation Time:

Cook Time: 15 minutes

Servings: 4

Ingredients

1/4 cup basil, chopped

1/4 cup parsley, chopped

3/4 pounds trimmed green beans

1 tablespoon ghee

1 minced garlic clove

3 diced bacon strips

salt, to taste

Instructions

1. Using a soup pot, boil some water then steam the green beans for 4 minutes until tenderized.

2. In the meantime, add the diced bacon into the fry pan and fry until crisp and golden brown.

3. Add the salt and garlic into the fry pan then cook until the garlic lightly browns then take the pan off the heat.

4. Drain the steamed beans and run under cold water then combine all the ingredients together and mix.

5. Serve immediately and enjoy as desired.

Nutrition Information

Calories: 63kcal | Fat: 3.7g | Carbohydrates: 7.4g | Protein: 2g

Broccolini Almonds Toast

Preparation Time: 5 minutes

Cook Time: 10 minutes

Servings: 2

Ingredients

1/8 teaspoon red pepper flakes

1/3 cup slivered almonds, toasted

1/2 teaspoon lime juice & zest

1 teaspoon minced garlic

1 tablespoon avocado oil

1 bunch trimmed broccolini

kosher salt, to taste

Instructions

1. Using a small skillet, add in the oil and heat over medium high heat.

2. Add the pepper flakes, garlic and stir cook for 3 minutes until tenderized.

3. Steam the trimmed broccolini until crisp tender or to taste.

4. Serve the broccolini garnished with the lime juice, zest and toasted almonds.

5. Sprinkle with the salt and enjoy.

Nutrition Information

Calories: 190kcal | Fat: 16.7g | Carbohydrates: 5g | Protein: 5.4g

MAIN DISH

Crock Pot Sirloin Roast

Preparation Time: 30 minutes

Cook Time: 8 hours

Servings: 2

Ingredients

1-pound bottom sirloin

1 teaspoon dried oregano

1 tablespoon ground turmeric

1 1/2 tablespoons apple cider vinegar

2 tablespoons sea salt

2 tablespoons avocado oil

3 tablespoons unsalted butter

Instructions

1. Combine the oregano, turmeric & salt together then use to season the sirloin.

2. Place the seasoned steak in the crock pot then coat with the avocado oil.

3. Add in the butter then cook until the steak is tenderized for 6-8 hours on low settings.

4. Shred once done cooking, glaze with the vinegar until fully covered.

5. Serve and enjoy as desired.

Nutrition Information

Calories: 329kcal | Fat: 33.5g | Carbohydrates: 2.9g | Protein:6.4g

Simple Fryer Tenders

Preparation Time: 5 minutes

Cook Time: 10 minutes

Servings: 4

Ingredients

1/2 cup almond flour

1 beaten egg

1 teaspoon paprika

1-pound chicken tenders

1 teaspoon powdered garlic

salt & pepper, to taste

Instructions

1. Coat the fryer basket with cooking oil spray.

2. Coat the chicken tenders with salt & pepper then run coated tenders through the flour, beaten egg and flour again.

3. Place the chicken tenders in the fryer basket then cook for 5 minutes at 350°F.

4. Flip the chicken tenders over then cook for an extra 5 minutes.

5. Serve and enjoy as desired.

Nutrition Information

Calories: 61kcal | Fat: 3.1g | Carbohydrates: 1.9g | Protein: 6.5g

Dressed Bacon Lettuce Wraps

Preparation Time: 15 minutes

Cook Time: 30 minutes

Servings: 4

Ingredients

for the lettuce wraps

1 butter lettuce head

1 cup halved cherry tomatoes

8 thick bacon slices

diced avocado, if desired

for the dressing

1/8 teaspoon powdered garlic

1/8 teaspoon powdered onion

1/4 cup almond milk

1 teaspoon chopped dill

1 tablespoon juiced lime

1 tablespoon chopped chives

1 tablespoon chopped dry parsley

1 1/2 cup mayonnaise

salt & pepper, to taste

Instructions

1. Prepare the baking sheet with parchment paper arrange the bacon slices in an even layer on the lined baking sheet.

2. Place the baking sheet in the oven and bake until crispy and golden brown for 20-30 minutes at 425°F then transfer onto kitchen towels to drain.

3. Using a mixing bowl, add the powdered garlic, onion, pepper, salt, chives, dill, parsley, lime juice, almond milk, mayonnaise and mix together until combined.

4. Serve the crispy bacon slices on the lettuce wraps then top with the diced avocado, cherry tomato and enjoy drizzled with the mayo dressing.

Nutrition Information

Calories: 422kcal | Fat: 26.9g | Carbohydrates: 6.4g | Protein: 9g

Thai Curry Beef

Preparation Time: 15 minutes

Cook Time: 5 hours

Servings: 4

Ingredients

1/4 cup beef broth

1/2 lemon juice & zest

3/4 teaspoon salt

1 teaspoon powdered turmeric

1 (14-ounce) can coconut cream

2 tablespoons Thai red curry paste

2 1/2 pounds cubed chuck steak

Instructions

1. Heat the oven up to 210°F then combine the beef broth, salt, curry paste and turmeric together in a mixing bowl.

2. Add in the lemon juice and zest then the coconut cream, chuck steak and combine until the meat is well coated.

3. Transfer the mixture into a baking pan then cover and bake in the oven for 2 hours.

4. Stir the mixture after 2 hours then return back into the oven and bake for another 1 1/2 hours until the steak is tenderized.

5. If the steak is yet to be softened, cook for an extra 30 minutes or until tender as desired then transfer into a bowl and set aside.

6. Return the pan back into the oven with the cooking juice and cook for 40 minutes at 320°F then return the meat back into the pan.

7. Serve and enjoy with veggies, noodles or rice.

Nutrition Information

Calories: 656kcal | Fat: 32.9g | Carbohydrates: 1.3g | Protein: 82.7g

Cauliflower Grits & Shrimp

Preparation Time: 2 minutes

Cook Time: 10 minutes

Servings: 2

Ingredients

for the shrimp

1 pound peeled & deveined shrimp

2 tablespoons ghee

3 tablespoons Cajun seasoning

kosher salt, to taste

for the grits

1 minced garlic clove

1 (12-ounce) bag frozen cauliflower

2 tablespoons ghee

kosher salt, to taste

Instructions

1. Using a medium sized saucepan, add in 2" water and boil.

2. Pour the cauliflower into a steamer basket then garnish with the garlic cloves, cover and steam until tenderized.

3. Once tender, transfer the garlic, cauliflower mix into a high speed blender, add in the ghee and blitz until chopped as desired.

4. Add in the salt, a little of the steaming water and process until a desired consistency is achieved.

5. In the meantime, pat dry the shrimp then generously coat with the Cajun seasoning and set aside.

6. Heat the tablespoons of ghee with a large skillet over medium high heat then add in the shrimp and cook for 2 minutes.

7. Flip the shrimp over and cook the other side for another 2 minutes until pink and deveined.

8. Serve the cauliflower grits, garnished with the deveined shrimps then top with the shrimp cooking juice and enjoy.

Nutrition Information

Calories: 510kcal | Fat: 33g | Carbohydrates: 3g | Protein: 47g

Mexican Crock Pot Beef

Preparation Time: 30 minutes

Cook Time: 7 hours 30 minutes

Servings: 4

Ingredients

1/2 cup water

1 teaspoon powdered chipotle

1 cup roughly chopped cilantro stems

2 teaspoons paprika

2 teaspoons ground cumin

2 teaspoons ground turmeric

2 teaspoons ground coriander

3 1/2 pounds beef short ribs

4 minced garlic cloves

salt & pepper, to taste

Instructions

1. Using a small mixing bowl, add in the dry ingredients and combine together.

2. Add the beef ribs into the crock pot then slightly rub each with the dry spice mixture.

3. Top the rubbed beef with the chopped cilantro, minced garlic and pour in some water.

4. Cook for 6-7 hours on low settings until tenderized then drain out the liquid.

5. Reduce the cooking liquid over medium heat for 10-15 minutes then pour it back into the crockpot.

6. Shred the beef and allow to soak in the liquid for a few minutes.

7. Serve and enjoy as desired.

Nutrition Information

Calories: 656kcal | Fat: 48.5g | Carbohydrates: 1.4g | Protein: 50.2g

Cajun Seasoned Fillets

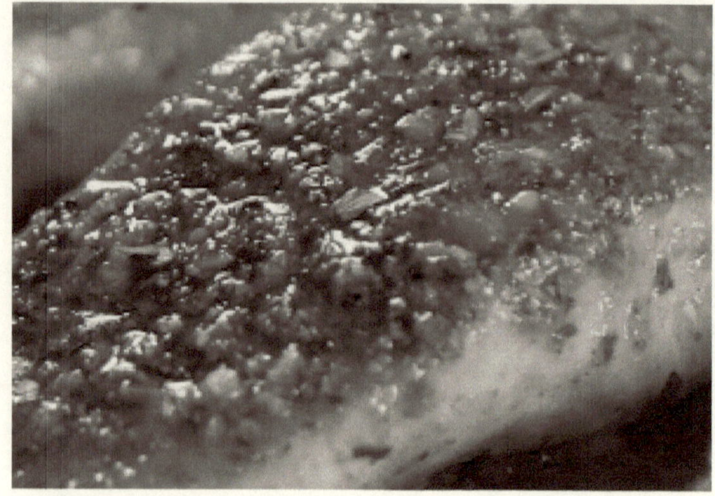

Preparation Time: 5 minutes

Cook Time: 10 minutes

Servings: 4

Ingredients

1 lime juice

2 tablespoons avocado oil

2 tablespoons Cajun seasoning

4 (4 ounce) catfish fillets

Instructions

1. Season the fillets with the Cajun then heat the avocado oil over medium high heat in a large skillet.

2. Add the fillets into the hot oil then cook for 5 minutes per side.

3. Serve with a garnish of the lime juice and enjoy.

Nutrition Information

Calories: 313kcal | Fat: 22.7g | Carbohydrates: 14.6g | Protein: 16g

Crab Bisque Meat

Preparation Time: 20 minutes

Cook Time: 25 minutes

Servings: 3

Ingredients

1-pound lump crab meet

1 tablespoon coconut oil

1 diced small onion

3 minced garlic cloves

1 diced red bell pepper

1/4 cup sherry, if desired

3 cups vegetable stock

2 cups coconut milk

salt, to taste

white & cayenne pepper, to taste

Instructions

1. Using a medium sized pot, add in the coconut oil and heat up over medium heat.

2. Add in the garlic, onion and sauté until translucent.

3. Add in the bell peppers and sauté for an extra minute then pour in the spices (except the salt) and stir together.

4. Pour in the coconut milk and simmer for 3 minutes then add in the vegetable stock and simmer again.

5. Add the crab meat and sherry into the pot and cook until the meat is heated through.

Nutrition Information

Calories: 158kcal | Fat: 11g | Carbohydrates: 4g | Protein: 11g

Air Fried Chicken Fillets

Preparation Time: 20 minutes

Cook Time: 15 minutes

Servings: 6

Ingredients

1/2 cup almond meal

1/2 teaspoon hot chili powder

1/2 cup finely grated parmesan cheese

1 large egg

1 teaspoon dried oregano

1 teaspoon powdered garlic

2 teaspoon celery salt

2 tablespoons heavy cream

2 pounds' chicken thigh fillets

Instructions

1. Slice each of the chicken thigh into 3 even sizes then place into a mixing bowl.

2. Add the dried oregano, chili powder, celery salt, powdered garlic and toss together until the chicken are well covered.

3. Transfer the bowl into the fridge and allow to marinate for an hour.

4. In the meantime, whisk the heavy cream and eggs together then use a separate bowl to combine the parmesan cheese and almond meal together.

5. Once the chicken is well marinated, dip each piece in the cream mixture then run through the flour mix until well coated then arranger in a fryer basket.

6. Fit the basket into the air fryer then air fry until golden brown for 6 minutes.

7. Repeat the same process for the remaining pieces then serve and enjoy as desired.

Nutrition Information

Calories: 359kcal | Fat: 18g | Carbohydrates: 1g | Protein: 44g

Simple Cheesy Pimento

Preparation Time: 10 minutes

Cook Time: 0 minute

Servings: 10

Ingredients

1/4 teaspoon seasoning

1/2 cup mayonnaise

1/2 package cream cheese

1 cup shredded sharp cheddar cheese

1 cup shredded Monterey jack cheese

2 teaspoons diced onion

3 tablespoons diced pimentos

salt & pepper, to taste

Instructions

1. Using a large mixing bowl, add in all the ingredients.

2. Use an electric mixer to combine the ingredients together until incorporated.

3. Serve and enjoy as desired.

Nutrition Information

Calories: 175kcal | Fat: 16.6g | Carbohydrates: 1.4g | Protein: 6.1g

Brussels & Bacon Sprouts

Preparation Time: 5 minutes

Cook Time: 25 minutes

Servings: 4

Ingredients

1/2 pound diced lean bacon

1 diced medium yellow onion

2 minced garlic cloves

2 pounds trimmed Brussels sprouts

2 cups chicken broth

4 tablespoons butter

salt & pepper, to taste

Instructions

1. Using a heavy duty pot, fry the bon dices over medium heat until crisp then drain on paper towels.

2. Add the garlic and onions into the pot and sauté for 3 minutes on low heat.

3. Add the Brussel sprouts into the pot and stir around until coated with the fat.

4. Season with the salt & pepper to taste.

5. Pour in the broth, cover the pot and cook until the sprouts are tenderized for 15 minutes over low heat.

6. Add in the butter and stir then dish out the sprouts.

7. Serve, garnished with the bacon dices and enjoy.

Nutrition Information

Calories: 316kcal | Fat: 14.6g | Carbohydrates: 24.1 | Protein: 22.8g

Cheesy Bacon Ball

Preparation Time: 20 minutes

Cook Time: 0 minute

Servings: 12

Ingredients

1/4 cup chopped fresh parsley

1/4 cup diced green onions

1/4 cup shredded blue cheese

1/2 cup milk

3/4 cup divided pecans

1 tablespoon poppy seeds

1 jar drained & diced pimento

1 package softened cream cheese

2 cups shredded sharp cheddar cheese

10 cooked bacon slices

salt & pepper, to taste

Instructions

1. Add the cream cheese into a mixing bowl and beat with a hand mixer until fluffy for a minute.

2. Add in the cheddar cheese, blue cheese, onions, half pecans and bacon then beat again for a minute until blended on high speed.

3. Season the mixture with the salt and pepper as desired.

4. Transfer the mixture into a plastic wrap and mold into a ball, then tighten and refrigerate for 2 hours.

5. Combine the remaining bacon, pecans, poppy seeds and parsley together then run the refrigerated cheese ball through the mixture until well coated.

6. Refrigerate the balls for another 30 minutes then serve and enjoy.

Nutrition Information

Calories: 205kcal | Fat: 17.8g | Carbohydrates: 3.7g | Protein: 9.2g

Chicken & Beef Loaf

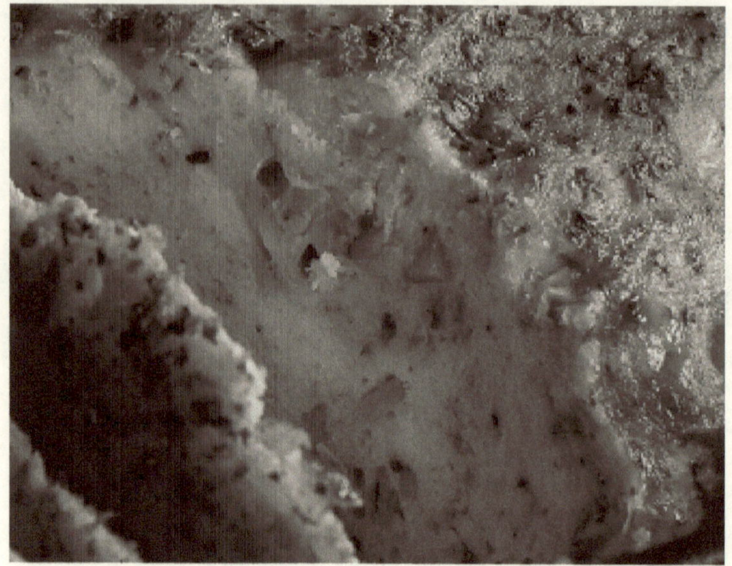

Preparation Time: 15 minutes

Cook Time: 1 hour

Servings: 2

Ingredients

1/3 cup ketchup

3/4 cup water

3/4 cup crushed pork rinds

1 envelope onion soup mix

1-pound ground beef

1-pound ground chicken breast

2 large eggs

2 bread loaf ends

Instructions

1. Heat the oven up to 350°F then combine all the ingredients together until incorporated.

2. Place the two ends of a bread loaf on the surface of a baking dish, end to end.

3. Mold the meat mixture into the loaf and on top of the other slice.

4. Top the mixture with extra ketchup then place in the oven and bake for an hour.

5. Allow the loaf cool off then slice and enjoy as desired.

Nutrition Information

Calories: 1122kcal | Fat: 46.6g | Carbohydrates: 36.9g | Protein: 94.1g

Broccoli Chicken Dish

Preparation Time: 5 minutes

Cook Time: 1 hour

Servings: 4

Ingredients

1/2 cup melted butter

1 family size bag frozen whole green beans 16-19 ounces

2 packages Italian dressing mix

4 chicken breasts, sliced into strips

a bunch of broccoli

Instructions

1. Using a large baking pan, arrange the broccoli in then place the chicken breast strips at the middle of the corn.

2. Pour the green beans along the other side of the pan then drizzle everything with the melted butter.

3. Sprinkle the entire mixture with the Italian dressing mix then cover with an aluminum foil.

4. Place the pan in the oven and bake until the broccoli and chicken cooked through for 1 hour at 350°F.

5. Serve and enjoy as desired.

Nutrition Information

Calories: 351kcal | Fat: 22.3g | Carbohydrates: 8.1g | Protein: 18.7g

Greek Potato Drumstick

Preparation Time: 20 minutes

Cook Time: 1 hour 30 minutes

Servings: 5

Ingredients

1/3 cup avocado oil

1/3 cup juiced lime

1 tablespoon dry oregano

2 teaspoons powdered garlic

4 pounds' chicken drumsticks

10 small red potato

kosher salt & black pepper, to taste

Instructions

1. Using a small mixing bowl, add in all the dry ingredients and stir together.

2. Wash the potatoes then dice in quarters.

3. Using a large baking dish, add in the quartered potatoes, chicken drumsticks and season.

4. Drizzle the seasoned drumsticks with the juiced lime, oil the cover with foil.

5. Bake the chicken for 1 hour at 350°F then remove the foil.

6. Bake, uncovered for an extra 30 minutes, this time at 400°F until slightly browned.

7. Serve and enjoy.

Nutrition Information

Calories: 811kcal | Fat: 36.9g | Carbohydrates: 45.5g | Protein: 72.2g

POULTRY RECIPES

Cheesy Lime Chicken Breast

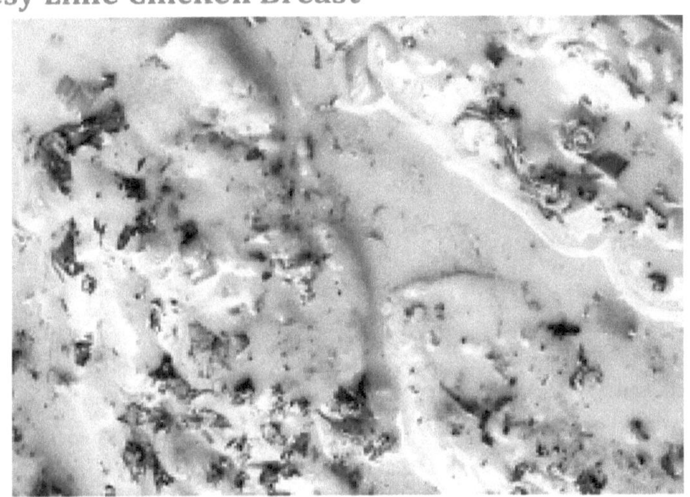

Preparation Time: 20 minutes

Cook Time: 30 minutes

Servings: 4

Ingredients

1/4 teaspoon dried basil

1/2 teaspoon salt

1/2 cup melted butter

1/2 cup shredded parmesan cheese

1 lime juice, with extra for garnishing

3 tablespoons mayonnaise

4 boneless skinless chicken breasts

Instructions

1. Add the chicken breasts into a Ziploc bag then pour in the lime juice, shake together and place in the refrigerator to marinate for an hour.

2. Add 1/4 cup of the melted butter into a large skillet then add in the marinated chicken and cook for 20 minutes until browned.

3. With a small mixing bowl, add in the basil, salt, parmesan cheese, mayonnaise, remaining butter and incorporate together.

4. Transfer the cooked chicken onto a baking sheet then top with the mayo mixture.

5. Transfer he baking sheet into the oven then bake for 10 minutes at 350°F until the cheese is melted.

6. Serve and enjoy with lime wedges as desired.

Nutrition Information

Calories: 1011kcal | Fat: 48.6g | Carbohydrates: 1.9g | Protein: 142.3g

Simple Chicken Breast Bowl

Preparation Time: 15 minutes

Cook Time: 20 minutes

Servings: 6

Ingredients

1 bottle of marinade

6 boneless & skinless chicken breasts

cooking oil spray

Instructions

1. Place the chicken breast into a Ziploc bag then pour in the marinade.

2. Massage the marinade into the chicken then transfer into the refrigerator to marinate for an hour.

3. Using a large skillet, coat it with the cooking oil spray then place over medium high heat until hot.

4. Add in the marinated chicken then cook for 10 minutes until browned.

5. Flip the chicken breast over and cook until done as desired.

6. Serve and enjoy to taste.

Nutrition Information

Calories: 360kcal | Fat: 8.4g | Carbohydrates: 1.6g | Protein: 69.3g

Buttered Chicken Fryer

Preparation Time: 25 minutes

Cook Time: 1 hour 35 minutes

Servings: 5

Ingredients

1/2 cup butter

1/2 teaspoon powdered garlic

1 teaspoon basil

1 teaspoon paprika

1 teaspoon parsley

5 pounds' chicken fryer

chopped assorted veggies

kosher salt & black pepper, to taste

Instructions

1. Heat the oven up to 425°F then melt the butter using a baking dish in the oven.

2. In the meantime, add all the seasonings into a small bowl then mix together.

3. Place the chicken into the melted butter in the pan and toss around until well coated with the butter.

4. Generously sprinkle the chicken with the seasoning mix, keep just a teaspoon aside.

5. Arrange the veggies around the chicken in the pan then sprinkle with the remaining seasoning.

6. Return the pan into the oven and bake for 1 1/2 hours, basting the chicken and veggies with regularly.

7. Serve and enjoy as desired.

Nutrition Information

Calories: 659kcal | Fat: 22.5g | Carbohydrates: 7.2g | Protein: 105.7g

Brown Rice Chicken Teriyaki

Preparation Time: 15 minutes

Cook Time: 30 minutes

Servings: 4

Ingredients

1/3 cup teriyaki sauce

1/2 teaspoon powdered garlic

1 tablespoon coconut oil

1-pound chicken breasts, boneless & skinless

2 cups broccoli

2 cups grated carrots

2 cups uncooked brown rice

Instructions

1. Add the oil into a large skillet then heat until hot over medium high heat.

2. Add the chicken breast into the skillet and stir cook for 7 minutes until slightly browned.

3. Add in the broccoli, teriyaki sauce, carrots, garlic powder and cook on medium heat for 10 minutes until tenderized.

4. Prepare the brown rice according to the packet instructions.

5. Serve the rice with the chicken vegetables and enjoy as desired.

Nutrition Information

Calories: 233kcal | Fat: 6.7g | Carbohydrates: 16.7g | Protein: 26.2g

Greens & Turkey Dish

Preparation Time: 30 minutes

Cook Time: 1 hour 45 minutes

Servings: 4

Ingredients

1 diced white onion

1 tablespoon coconut oil

1 teaspoon red pepper flakes

1 large smoked turkey leg, cooked

3 cups chicken broth

3 minced garlic cloves

32 oz. collard greens, chopped

hot sauce, to taste

salt & pepper, to taste

Instructions

1. Using a large skillet, add in the oil and heat over medium heat.

2. Add the onions into the oil and cook until tenderized then add in the garlic and cook until fragrant.

3. Add in the smoked turkey, red pepper flakes, chicken broth and bring to a boil.

4. Reduce the heat then boil on a low for 30 minutes then set aside to cool.

5. Remove the bone from the cooled meat, chop into pieces then return back into the pot.

6. Allow the bone to simmer for 10 minutes then add in the chopped greens and wilt.

7. Cover the pot and allow to simmer for 40-50 minutes or until a desired texture is achieved.

8. Season with salt & pepper to taste then serve and enjoy with the hot sauce.

Nutrition Information

Calories: 349kcal | Fat: 19.5g | Carbohydrates: 23.3g| Protein: 12.5g

Simple Smokehouse Chicken

Preparation Time: 15 minutes

Cook Time: 1 hour 50 minutes

Servings: 5

Ingredients

1 tablespoon hot sauce

1 teaspoon smoked paprika

1 whole chicken, bone & skin in

1 teaspoon crushed red pepper flakes

1 cups cider vinegar, with extra 1/2 cup

3 tablespoons brown sugar

kosher salt & smoked black pepper, to taste

Instructions

1. Using a Dutch oven, add in all the ingredients except the chicken and stir together until the sugar is dissolved.

2. Bake the chicken in the oven skin side down for 45 minutes at 300°F then flip and cook for another 45 minutes.

3. Remove the lid and broil until browned and crispy for 20 minutes.

4. Serve and enjoy, drizzled with extra cooking juice and enjoy as desired.

Nutrition Information

Calories: 46kcal | Fat:2g | Carbohydrates: 8.5g | Protein: 2.1g

Creamy Cornbread Dressed Chicken

Preparation Time: 30 minutes

Cook Time: 1 hour

Servings: 8

Ingredients

1/2 cup diced onions

1/2 cup chicken broth

1 cup shredded chicken

1 tablespoon avocado oil

1 pan crumbled cornbread

1 tablespoon ground sage

1 (10 ounces) can cream of chicken soup

2 boiled & diced eggs

2 chopped celery stalks

salt & pepper, to taste

Instructions

1. Bake the corn bread until toasted for 20-30 minutes at 300°F, stirring just once then set aside to cool off.

2. In the meantime add the oil into a saucepan and heat over medium high heat.

3. Add in the celery, onions and cook, stirring constantly over medium high heat until tenderized.

4. Pour in the chicken soup, chicken broth, seasoning and stir then reduce the heat to a medium and stir cook until well incorporated.

5. take the pan off the heat then add in the shredded chicken, diced eggs and stir.

6. With a large separate bowl, add in the toasted cornbread then cover with the shredded chicken sauce and stir until coated.

7. Transfer the entire mixture into a baking dish then bake until lightly browned for 30-35 minutes at 350°F.

8. Serve and enjoy as desired.

Nutrition Information

Calories: 193kcal | Fat: 7.5g | Carbohydrates: 23.6g | Protein: 5.1g

A Single Pan Chicken Teriyaki

Preparation Time: 20 minutes

Cook Time: 30 minutes

Servings: 4

Ingredients

2 diced green onions

2 pounds boneless skinless chicken breasts

3 cups broccoli florets

3 cups cauliflower florets

for the sauce

1/2 cup teriyaki sauce

1 teaspoon siracha

2 tablespoons honey

Instructions

1. Coat a baking sheet with cooking oil spray and set aside.

2. Dice the chicken breast into bits then chop the cauliflower and broccoli into florets.

3. With a small mixing bowl, combine all the sauce ingredients then place the vegetable and chicken breast on a baking sheet.

3. Drizzle the chicken and vegetable with the sauce mixture and toss together until coated then place in the oven and bake for 30 minutes at 375°F until the veggies are tenderized and the chicken done to taste.

4. Serve and enjoy as desired.

Nutrition Information

Calories: 1658kcal | Fat: 110.4g | Carbohydrates: 113g | Protein: 58.9g

Cheese & Broccoli Filled Chicken Breasts

Preparation Time: 25 minutes

Cook Time: 30 minutes

Servings: 6

Ingredients

1/4 teaspoon paprika

1/2 teaspoon powdered onion

1 1/2 teaspoons powdered garlic, divided

3 large skinless & boneless chicken breasts

salt & black pepper, to taste

for the stuffing

1/2 cup chopped bell pepper

1 tablespoon mayonnaise

1 cup shredded cheddar cheese

1 cup diced fresh broccoli florets

3 tablespoons avocado oil

Instructions

1. Heat the oven up to 425°F then use a small mixing bowl to combine 1/2 of the powdered garlic, pepper, salt, paprika and powdered onion.

2. Transfer the chicken breast onto a chopping board then press down on each piece and carefully cut a pocket into the chicken piece.

3. Using a microwavable bowl, add in 2 tablespoons water, broccoli florets and microwave until tenderized for 3 minutes on high setting then drain off excess water.

4. Add the mayonnaise, cheddar cheese, bell pepper, remaining garlic powder and stir together until incorporated.

5. Stuff each of the chicken pockets with 1/2 of the broccoli florets mixture.

6. Combine the powdered garlic, onion powder, pepper, paprika, salt and combine together then sprinkle over each side of the chicken breast.

7. Add some cooking oil into an oven proof skillet and heat until hot over medium high heat.

8. Carefully place the chicken breast in the hot oil and cook until browned for 5 minutes per side.

9. Remove from the eye then transfer the entire skillet into the oven and cook until cooked through for 10-15 minutes.

10. Allow the chicken to cool off for a bit then serve and enjoy as desired.

Nutrition Information

Calories: 666kcal | Fat: 29g | Carbohydrates: 23.7g | Protein: 77.7g

Low Carb Southern Chicken

Preparation Time: 13 minutes

Cook Time: 20 minutes

Servings: 6

Ingredients

1 teaspoon paprika

1 cup coconut flour

1 teaspoon powdered garlic

5 pounds' chicken leg quarters

salt & pepper, to taste

cooking oil, for frying

Instructions

1. Using a large mixing bowl, add in the paprika, powdered garlic, pepper, salt, chicken and combine together until the chicken is well coated.

2. Cover the mixing bowl and allow the chicken to marinate for an hour in the refrigerator.

3. Cover the marinated chicken with the flour and massage well.

4. Heat the cooking oil in a large skillet over medium high heat then add in the chicken and cook in batches until golden brown and crisp for 8 minutes per side.

5. Serve and enjoy as desired.

Nutrition Information

Calories: 425kcal | Fat: 32g | Carbohydrates: 1g | Protein: 34g

Slow Cooked Lettuce Wrapped Chicken

Preparation Time: 10 minutes

Cook Time: 3-7 hours

Servings: 4

Ingredients

1/2 cup honey

1/2 cup soy sauce

1 tablespoon coconut oil

1 tablespoon minced garlic

4 boneless skinless chicken breasts

for serving

lettuce leaves

a bunch of green onions

Instructions

1. Using a small mixing bowl, add in the sesame oil, garlic, honey, soy sauce then stir together.

2. Place the chicken breast in a crock pot then cover with the honey sauce and toss to coat.

3. Cook on high setting for 2-3 hours or 6-7 hours on low settings.

4. Take the chicken breast out of the pot and into a mixing bowl then shred into pieces.

5. Return the shredded chicken back into the pot, stir into the cooking sauce and well coated.

6. Serve the sauced chicken breast into the lettuce leaves then top with the diced onions, roll up and enjoy.

Nutrition Information

Calories: 864kcal | Fat: 17.8g | Carbohydrates: 37.1g | Protein: 142g

BEEF & PORK RECIPES

Succulent Swiss Steak

Preparation Time: 10 minutes

Cook Time: 5-9 hours

Servings: 4

Ingredients

1/2 teaspoon powdered garlic

1 diced onion

1 teaspoon smoked paprika

2 teaspoons oregano

2 pounds cubed steak

15 ounces' tomato sauce

15 ounces diced canned tomatoes

salt & pepper, to taste

Instructions

1. Using a slow cooker, add in the cubed steak and garnish with the diced onions.

2. With a large mixing bowl, add in the tomato sauce, diced tomatoes, all the seasoning and combine together.

3. Pour the tomato mixture over the cubed steaks in the crock pot.

4. Cover the crock pot and cook for 4-5 hours on high settings or 7-9 hours on low settings.

5. Serve and enjoy with rice, potatoes or noodles and enjoy.

Nutrition Information

Calories: 393kcal | Fat: 9.2g | Carbohydrates: 8.6 | Protein: 65.4

Simple Beef Steaks

Preparation Time: 15 minutes

Cook Time: 20 minutes

Servings: 2

Ingredients

1 cup beef broth

2 tablespoons coconut oil

plain flour

ground beef

diced sweet onion

Instructions

1. Add the coconut oil into large skillet and heat.

2. Form the ground beef into small patties then run each piece through the plain flour.

3. Transfer the flour coated beef into the heated oil in the skillet and cook over medium heat until browned on each side.

4. Add in the sweet onions and cook until lightly browned then pour in the beef broth, cover and cook for 10 minutes.

5. Serve the prepared ground beef and enjoy as desired.

Nutrition Information

Calories: 595kcal | Fat: 39.3g | Carbohydrates: 9.9g | Protein: 50.2g

Oven Beef Kabobs

Preparation Time: 20 minutes

Cook Time: 30 minutes

Servings: 4

Ingredients

1 bottle of marinade

1-pound cherry tomatoes

1 pound of cored & seeded bell peppers, diced into 1" pieces

2 pounds' sirloin

2 peeled & diced onions

Instructions

1. Dice the sirloin beef into bite sized cubes then place into a zip lock bag.

2. Pour a cup of the marinade into the zip lock bag then zip and allow to marinate for an hour.

3. Heat the oven up to 350°F then soak 10 wooden skewers.

4. Sew the marinated beef, tomatoes and peppers onto the skewers then transfer onto a rimmed baking sheet.

5. Bake the kabobs for 30 minutes at 350°F, turning every 10 minutes until browned.

6. Serve and enjoy as desired.

Nutrition Information

Calories: 499kcal | Fat: 22g | Carbohydrates: 5.3g | Protein: 44.1g

Slow Cooked BBQ Ribs

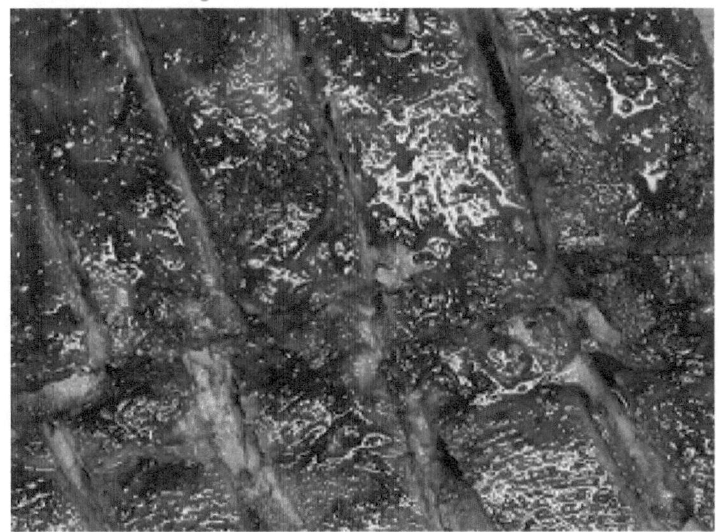

Preparation Time: 10 minutes

Cook Time: 8 hours 10 minutes

Servings: 3

Ingredients

1/4 teaspoon stevia powder

1/2 teaspoon salt

1/2 cup pressed tomatoes

1/2 teaspoon black pepper

1/2 teaspoon cayenne pepper

1 tablespoon liquid smoke

1 tablespoon smoked paprika

1 tablespoon Worcestershire sauce

2 minced garlic cloves

38 ounces ribs rack

sugarless BBQ sauce

Instructions

1. Using a medium mixing bowl, combine the BBQ sauce with the remaining ingredients (except the rack of ribs).

2. Transfer the rack of ribs into a crock pot then cover with the BBQ sauce mixture.

3. Cook on high setting for 4 hours or 8 hours on low setting.

4. Transfer the cooked ribs onto a baking tray then drizzle with the sauce from the crockpot.

5. Place the tray in the oven and bake until crispy for 10 minutes.

6. Chop the ribs as desired, serve and enjoy.

Nutrition Information

Calories: 804kcal | Fat: 62.94g | Carbohydrates: 4.33g | Protein: 46.37g

Baked Herbal Crusted Ham

Preparation Time: 10 minutes

Cook Time: 15 minutes

Servings: 2

Ingredients

1/2 cup mayonnaise

1 smoked ham

1 cup prepared mustard

2 tablespoons minced garlic

2 tablespoon chopped rosemary

freshly ground pepper

Instructions

1. Using a small mixing bowl, add in all the ingredients (except the ham) and incorporate together.

2. Arrange the ham on a roasting pan with the fat side up and cover with the mayonnaise mixture.

3. Transfer the pan into the oven and bake for 15 minutes at 300°F.

4. Serve and enjoy the ham as desired.

Nutrition Information

Calories: 481kcal | Fat: 46.7g | Carbohydrates: 8.4g | Protein: 10.2g

Creamy Pork Chops

Preparation Time: 20 minutes

Cook Time: 25 minutes

Servings: 4

Ingredients

1/2 cup heavy cream

1 cup chicken broth

3 tablespoons melted butter

4 boneless pork chops

salt & pepper, to taste

Instructions

1. Place a large skillet over medium high heat then add in the butter, heating until hot.

2. Add in the pork chops, with a sprinkle of salt, pepper and cook until browned, flipping halfway through the cook time.

3. Pour in the chicken broth then reduce the heat to a medium and cook for 10 minutes until the broth is almost evaporated.

4. Once the broth is cooked, remove the pork chops then pour in the heavy cream into the skillet and stir cook for a few minutes until incorporated, thick and warm.

5. Serve the pork and enjoy sauced with the warm cream mixture.

Nutrition Information

Calories: 349kcal | Fat: 24.6g | Carbohydrates: 0.9g | Protein: 27.3g

Crock Pot Pulled Pork

Preparation Time: 5 minutes

Cook Time: 8 hours

Servings: 8

Ingredients

1/2 teaspoon cumin

1 teaspoon salt

1 juiced orange

1 teaspoon pepper

1 teaspoon oregano

1 diced yellow onion

2 tablespoons paprika

4 minced garlic cloves

4 1/2 pounds' pork shoulder

Instructions

1. Add the orange juice, minced garlic and diced onion into a crock pot.

2. With a small mixing bowl, add in all the spices and mix together.

3. Trim the pork shoulder off the excess fat then rub with the spice mixture then place into the crock pot.

4. Cook for 8 hours on low settings then shred one done.

5. Serve and enjoy as desired.

Nutrition Information

Calories: 251kcal | Fat: 11g | Carbohydrates: 4g | Protein: 13g

Beef & Cabbage Sheet Pan

Preparation Time: 20 minutes

Cook Time: 20 minutes

Servings: 4

Ingredients

1 cabbage head, cut into 1" slices

2 pounds' stew meat

coconut oil

for the seasonings mixture

1/2 teaspoon pepper

1 tablespoon paprika

1 teaspoon powdered onion

1 teaspoon powdered garlic

kosher salt & cayenne pepper, to taste

Instructions

1. Heat the oven up to 400°F then coat a baking sheet with the coconut oil.

2. Add the cabbage slices on a side of the baking sheet and the stew meat on the other side.

3. Drizzle the veggies and meat with extra oil and toss well until coated then sprinkle with the seasoning mixture.

4. Bake the meat & veggies with until the browned and done as desired for 20-30 minutes at 400°F.

5. Serve and enjoy as desired.

Nutrition Information

Calories: 146kcal | Fat: 5.2g | Carbohydrates: 21.2g | Protein: 9.1g

RICE, NOODLES & PASTA RECIPES

Zucchini Shrimp Scampi

Preparation Time: 15 minutes

Cook Time: 20 minutes

Servings: 2

Ingredients

1 lemon zest & wedges

2 tablespoons ghee

2 diced garlic cloves

2 tablespoons avocado oil

2 spiralized medium zucchini

6 deveined jumbo shrimp

salt, to taste

a handful of parsley

diced green onion, to serve

Instructions

1. Using a wide saucepan, add in the ghee and heat over medium heat.

2. Add the shrimp in batches into the hot ghee to allow enough space between each and cook for 2 minutes per side then set aside.

3. Add the diced garlic into the pan and sauté until tenderized for 2 minutes then add in the chopped zucchini and cook until tender for 2 minutes.

4. Return the shrimps back into the pan then take the pan off the heat.

5. Pour in the avocado oil, lemon zest and stir together.

6. Serve with a garnish of diced onions, parsley and lemon wedges squeeze.

7. Season with the oil to taste and enjoy.

Nutrition Information

Calories: 335kcal | Fat: 26.1g | Carbohydrates: 6.1g | Protein: 19g

Piccata Shrimp Pasta

Preparation Time: 10 minutes

Cook Time: 20 minutes

Servings: 4

Ingredients

1/4 teaspoon powdered garlic

1/2 lime zest

1/2 cup juiced lime

1/2 cup chicken stock

1 sliced thin lime

1 sliced thin shallot

1 pound peeled & deveined shrimp

2 tablespoons butter

2 minced garlic cloves

3 tablespoons capers

4 tablespoons ghee

4 spiralized medium zucchinis

chopped fresh parsley, to serve

kosher salt & black pepper, to taste

Instructions

1. Cover the spiralized zucchini with kitchen towels, set aside and allow to drain for some minutes.

2. Place a large sauté pan over medium heat then add in the butter and melt.

3. In the meantime, rub the shrimp with the powdered garlic, salt then place into the sauté pan and cook until pink for 2 minutes on each side then remove from the pan.

4. Add the shallot and garlic into the pan then sauté until fragrant and translucent for 3 minutes

5. Add the ghee into the pan then melt and add in the chicken stock, lime juice, zest and bring to a low boil.

6. Add in the capers, sliced lime and cook on low heat until the slices become tender for 5 minutes.

7. Return the shrimps back into the pan then add in the zoodles, toss and cook until the shrimp is heated through and the zoodles tenderized for 3 minutes.

8. Serve with a sprinkle of black pepper, garnished with parsley and enjoy.

Nutrition Information

Calories: 326kcal | Fat: 22g | Carbohydrates: 5.9g | Protein: 24.7g

Carbonara Bacon Zucchini Noodles

Preparation Time: 20 minutes

Cook Time: 25 minutes

Servings: 4

Ingredients

1/4 cup chicken broth

1/2 teaspoon turmeric

1 cup diced bacon

1 cup butternut squash

2 cups cauliflower

2 tablespoons coconut oil

3 cups spiralized zucchini

3 tablespoons melted butter

salt, to taste

a handful of fresh sage leaves

Instructions

1. Using a sauce pan over medium heat, steam the cauliflower and butternut squash until heated through

2. Pour the coconut oil into fry pan the fry the diced bacon until crispy and golden then set aside.

3. Add the sage leaves into the fry pan and cook until crispy then transfer into the bacon bowl.

4. Steam the zucchini noodles in the sauce pan until cooked to taste.

5. Add the steamed cauliflower, squash, turmeric, ghee, salt and 2 tablespoons broth into a high speed blender and process until creamy and smooth as desired.

6. Serve the prepared zoodles then top with the creamy sauce with a garnish of the sage leaves and bacon pieces and enjoy with a sprinkle of salt and enjoy.

Nutrition Information

Calories: 397kcal | Fat: 29.5g | Carbohydrates: 17.5g | Protein: 18.5g

Thai Noodles Shrimp

Preparation Time: 20 minutes

Cook Time: 20 minutes

Servings: 4

Ingredients

1/4 cup chopped cilantro

1/4 teaspoon crushed red pepper

1 juiced lemon

1 minced garlic clove

1 teaspoon cashew butter

1 1/2 tablespoons divide avocado oil

2 beaten large eggs

2 chopped green onions

2 tablespoons coconut aminos

2 (7 ounce) pack fettuccini noodles

4 crushed cashews

18 medium shrimp

sea salt, to taste

Instructions

1. Prepare the noodles according to the packet instructions then set aside.

2. With a small mixing bowl, add in 3/4 tablespoon oil, 1/2 lemon juice, coconut aminos, red pepper, garlic, cashew butter, combine and then set aside.

3. Place a large skillet over medium heat then add in the remaining oil and cook the shrimp seasoned with salt for 2 minutes per side until pink.

4. Move the shrimp to a side of the skillet then pour the beaten egg into the middle and scramble cook for a minute.

5. Add in the prepared noodles, cilantro, sauce mixture, onion and toss everything together until mix then allow to heat through.

6. Adjust the seasoning to taste then serve drizzled with the remain lemon juice, garnish with cashews and enjoy.

Nutrition Information

Calories: 180kcal | Fat: 12g | Carbohydrates: 5g | Protein: 12g

Chicken Breast Noodles Soup

Prep Time: 10 minutes

Cook Time: 15 minutes

Servings: 4

Ingredients

1/2 teaspoon basil, dried

1/2 teaspoon oregano, dried

3/4 cup green onion, diced

1 cup celery, diced

1 cup carrots, diced

1 pound boneless & skinless chicken breast

2 tablespoons avocado oil

2 cups spiralized noodles

6 cups chicken stock

sea salt & ground pepper, to taste

Instructions

1. Using a large saucepan, add in the coconut and heat over medium heat then add in the chicken breast and cook until almost cooked through for 15 minutes.

2. Shred the chicken breast then add in the onion, carrots, celery and cook for an extra 5 minutes.

3. Add in the remaining ingredients then cover the pan and boil.

4. Reduce the heat and allow to a simmer for 25 minutes.

5. In the meantime, prepare the noodles according to the packet instructions.

6. Add the prepared noodles into the simmered soup allow to heat through and blend then serve and enjoy as desired.

Nutrition Information

Calories: 263kcal | Fat: 8.5g | Carbohydrates: 17g | Protein: 28.2g

Cauliflower Chicken Rice Soup

Preparation Time: 5 minutes

Cook Time: 30 minutes

Servings: 6

Ingredients

1/4 cup fresh parsley

1 bay leaf

1 diced small onion

1 teaspoon fresh thyme

1 boneless & skinless chicken thigh

2 diced carrots

2 tablespoons ghee

2 diced celery stalks

2 cups riced cauliflower

2 cups canned full fat coconut milk

4 cups chicken broth

salt & pepper, to taste

Instructions

1. Using a large soup pot, add in the ghee and melt then add in the celery, carrots, onion and cook until tenderized for 8 minutes.

2. Season the veggies with salt, pepper then add in the thyme and stir.

3. Pour the chicken broth in, add the bay leaf and boil then simmer on low heat.

4. Add in the chicken thighs and simmer until the chicken is cooked through.

5. Take the chicken out of the pot and shred then dispose the bay leaf.

6. Place the shredded chicken back into the pot then add in the riced cauliflower and simmer until the rice is cooked.

7. Pour in the coconut milk, parsley and cook until heated through.

8. Serve and enjoy with a season of salt & pepper as desired.

Nutrition Information

Calories: 265kcal | Fat: 17g | Carbohydrates: 11.7g | Protein: 6.1g

Riced Cauliflower with Bacon & Shrimp

Preparation Time: 15 minutes

Cook Time: 30 minutes

Servings: 5

Ingredients

for the shrimp

1/2 chopped bell pepper

1/2 tablespoon minced garlic

1 tablespoon butter

1 tablespoon creole seasoning

1 pound peeled & deveined shrimp

2 teaspoons paprika

4 bacon slices

a pinch of salt

for the cauliflower

1/4 cup heavy cream

1/2 cup unsweetened almond milk

1 cup shredded sharp cheddar cheese

2 tablespoons butter

2 tablespoons tomato paste

2 sliced green onions, if desired

2 tablespoons crumbled goat cheese, if desired

4 cups cauliflower rice

for the sauce

1/4 cup heavy cream

1/2 cup low salt vegetable broth

1 teaspoon Worcestershire sauce

1 teaspoon tabasco sauce, if desired

2 tablespoon cream cheese

Instructions

1. Using a small mixing bowl, add in the paprika, salt, creole seasoning and toss in the shrimp until well coated.

2. Using a large skillet, add in the bacon slices and cook until crisp over medium high heat then crumble and set aside.

3. Reserve a tablespoon of the bacon juice then add in the minced garlic, tablespoon butter and cook for 30 seconds then add in the chopped peppers and tenderized.

4. Add in the shrimp and cook for 5 minutes until done take the shrimp, pepper out of the skillet and set aside.

5. Combine all the sauce ingredients together and simmer until reduced by 1/4.

6. Add the tomato paste, heavy cream, almond milk and butter into a saucepan and heat until a low boil is reached then stir in the cheese until melted.

7. Add the riced cauliflower into the sauce pan and stir then simmer over low heat until done as desired.

8. Serve the cauliflower rice with the shrimp, drizzled with sauce and garnished with the bacon, goat cheese and green onions.

Nutrition Information

Calories: 415kcal | Fat: 26g | Carbohydrates: 8g | Protein: 31g

Chicken Rice Noodles Lettuce Wraps

Preparation Time: 20 minutes

Cook Time: 25 minutes

Servings: 3

Ingredients

1 cup baby mushrooms, diced

2 tablespoons brown sugar

3 tablespoons soy sauce

3 diced green onions

3 diced boneless skinless chicken breasts

rice sticks

cooking oil for the rice

a small bunch of lettuce head

a small can water chestnuts, diced

Instructions

1. Using a large skillet, add in a tablespoon of oil and heat over medium heat.

2. Add in the chicken breast and stir cook until cooked through.

3. Using a large mixing bowl, add in the brown sugar, soy sauce, combine then add in the diced chestnuts, mushrooms, onions, cooked chicken and combine.

4. Pour the chicken vegetables back into the skillet then stir in the sauce and stir cook over medium heat until heated through.

5. Using a sauté pan, pour in the cooking oil and heat for several minutes over medium heat then break in the rice sticks and transfer onto paper towels immediately.

6. Serve the chicken vegetables in the lettuce leaves, top with the rice sticks, serve and enjoy as desired.

Nutrition Information

Calories: 933kcal | Fat: 15.1g | Carbohydrates: 56.1g | Protein: 144.4g

Beef, Rice & Broccoli Florets

Preparation Time: 20 minutes

Cook Time: 25 minutes

Servings: 4

Ingredients

1/4 cup soy sauce

1/4 teaspoon black pepper

1-pound broccoli florets

1-pound sirloin, sliced into thin strips

2 tablespoons cornstarch

2 teaspoons minced garlic

3 tablespoons olive oil

brown rice

Instructions

1. Add 2 tablespoons of oil into a large skillet and heat over medium high heat.

2. Using a medium sized mixing bowl, add in the cornstarch, pepper and combine together.

3. Adding the sirloin strips and toss around until the strips are fully coated.

4. Transfer the coated strips into the hot oil in the skillet and cook for 5 minutes until slightly browned.

5. Take the beef out of the skillet, set aside and reduce the heat to a medium then pour in the remaining oil.

6. Add in the broccoli florets, garlic and cook for 5 minutes until tenderized.

7. Add the beef back into the skillet then pour in 1/3 cup water, soy sauce and cook, for 4 minutes until thickened.

8. Prepare the brown rice according to the packet instructions.

9. Serve the rice along with the broccoli beef and enjoy.

Nutrition Information

Calories: 1062kcal | Fat: 23.6g | Carbohydrates: 139.6g | Protein: 66g

SALAD, SIDES & SOUP RECIPES

Simple Low Carb Coleslaw

Preparation Time: 10 minutes

Cook Time:

Servings: 6

Ingredients

1/2 cup mayonnaise

1/2 teaspoon celery seed, if desired

1 grated carrot

1 tablespoon swerve

1 chopped cabbage head

1 teaspoon dijon mustard

1 tablespoon juiced lime

1 tablespoon apple cider vinegar

salt & pepper, to taste

Instructions

1. Using a mixing bowl, add in the pepper, salt, swerve, celery seed, mustard, juiced lime, vinegar, mayo and combine together.

2. Toss the grated carrots and cabbage with the vinegar mix until well coated.

3. Serve and enjoy as desired.

Nutrition Information

Calories: 178kcal | Fat: 14g | Carbohydrates: 13g | Protein: 3g

Simple Sausage Pepper Gravy

Preparation Time: 5 minutes

Cook Time: 15 minutes

Servings: 8

Ingredients

1/8 teaspoon red pepper flakes

1/2 teaspoon xanthan gum

1-pound ground sausage

1 cup low salt chicken stock

1 tablespoon fresh sage leaves

2 cups heavy cream

sea salt & black pepper, to taste

Instructions

1. Using a large skillet, heat the oil over medium high heat then add in the sausage and cook until brown and cooked through, crumbling into smaller chunks then drain off excess fat.

2. Reduce the heat to medium low then sprinkle the crumbled sausage with the xanthan gum, red pepper flakes, sage and stir together.

3. Add in the stock in bits then increase the heat to a medium and bring the mixture to a simmer, stirring until the mixture thickens.

4. Pour in the heavy cream and stir, then simmer again, continually stirring.

5. Simmer on low until the mixture is thickened again then season with the salt & pepper to taste.

6. Serve and enjoy as desired.

Nutrition Information

Calories: 396kcal | Fat: 38g | Carbohydrates: 3g | Protein: 12g

Cherry, Kale & Broccoli Salad

Preparation Time: 20 minutes

Cook Time: 0 minute

Servings: 5

Ingredients

1/2 cup canola oil

1/2 cup vinegar cider

1/2 cup dried cherries

1/2 cup sunflower kernels

3 cups broccoli florets

5 tablespoons maple syrup

8 cups kale, chopped

salt & pepper, to taste

Instructions

1. Using a large mixing bowl, add in the dry cherries, kernels, broccoli, kale and set aside.

2. Using a mason jar, add in the pepper, salt, maple syrup, oil then cover and shake until incorporated.

3. Pour the maple mixture over the cherries mix and toss together to coat.

4. Serve and enjoy as desired or refrigerate for later.

Nutrition Information

Calories: 467kcal | Fat: 30.9g | Carbohydrates: 40.4g | Protein: 8.8g

Simple Paleo Coleslaw

Preparation Time: 15 minutes

Cook Time: 0 minute

Servings: 6

Ingredients

1/4 teaspoon ground mustard

1/2 Cup mayonnaise

1/2 cup grated carrots

1 cup shredded red cabbage

1 tablespoon chopped parsley

1 1/2 tablespoons honey

2 tablespoons apple cider vinegar

5 cup shredded green cabbage

salt, to taste

Instructions

1. Using a large mixing bowl, add in the mustard, honey, vinegar, mayonnaise and whisk together until smooth.

2. Season with salt & pepper to taste then add in the carrot, cabbages, parsley and toss together until fully combined.

3. Serve and enjoy.

Nutrition Information

Calories: 168kcal | Fat: 13.9g | Carbohydrates: 10.4g | Protein: 1.5g

Floury Cream Vegetable Soup

Preparation Time: 20 minutes

Cook Time: 30 minutes

Servings: 6

Ingredients

1/4 cup melted butter

1/2 cup water

1 cup heavy cream

1 diced large onion

1 tablespoon fresh parsley

1 tablespoon plain flour, if desired

26 ounces frozen mixed vegetables

40 ounces' chicken broth

salt & pepper, to taste

Instructions

1. Add the melted butter into a Dutch oven over medium high heat then sauté the diced onions for 5 minutes until tenderized.

2. Pour the mixed vegetables and chicken broth into the oven and boil then simmer for 10 minutes until tenderized.

3. Add in the pepper, parsley, salt, heavy cream and stir in, simmering until heated through.

4. Combine the plain flour with the cup of water until the flour is fully dissolved.

5. Pour the flour mix into the soup, stir and continue to simmer for 10 more minutes.

6. Serve and enjoy, as desired.

Nutrition Information

Calories: 583kcal | Fat: 21.1g | Carbohydrates: 11.1g | Protein: 35g

Buttery Green Beans

Preparation Time: 15 minutes

Cook Time: 25-30 minutes

Servings: 1

Ingredients

1 butter stick

fresh green beans

salt & pepper, to taste

Instructions

1. Trim the ends of the beans off and dispose then break each into bite sizes.

2. Add the beans pieces into a large pot along with the butter and fill with some water.

3. Turn the heat up to medium high and bring the beans to a boil, until tenderized, occasionally stirring.

4. Season with salt & pepper to taste and serve, enjoying as desired.

Nutrition Information

Calories: 343kcal | Fat: 30.4g | Carbohydrates: 10.7g | Protein: 3.5g

Simple Keto Beef Soup

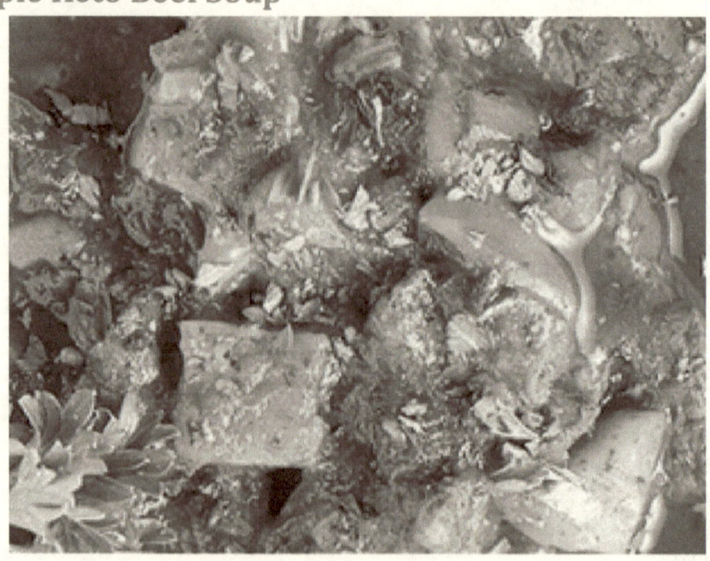

Preparation Time: 25 minutes

Cook Time: 50 minutes

Servings: 4

Ingredients

1/2 teaspoon basil, dried

1 teaspoon minced garlic

1 tablespoon Italian seasoning, dried

2 cups prepared ground beef

2 (14 ounce) cans tomato sauce

Instructions

1. Add all the ingredients into a sauce pot and stir.

2. Place the pot over medium heat and boil.

3. Reduce the heat to a simmer until the sauce is thickened.

4. Serve and enjoy as desired.

Nutrition Information

Calories: 118kcal | Fat: 3.3g | Carbohydrates: 13.1g | Protein: 9g

Collard Greens Stew

Preparation Time: 5 minutes

Cook Time: 40 minutes

Servings: 5

Ingredients

1 diced onion

1 melted stick butter

2 cups water

2 pounds stemmed collards, chopped into 1/2" strips

8 diced bacon strips

salt & hot sauce, as desired

Instructions

1. Using a large saucepan, cook the bacon strips over medium high heat for 5 minutes until crisp.

2. Add in the melted butter, onion and cook for 5 extra minutes until tenderized.

3. Add in the cups of water and allow to simmer for 10 minutes.

4. Add in the collards leaves and cook for 20 minutes until tenderized.

5. Serve, seasoned with the salt, sauce and enjoy.

Nutrition Information

Calories: 155kcal | Fat: 10.2g | Carbohydrates: 10.3g | Protein: 6.8g

Ground Beef Zucchini Goulash

Preparation Time: 25 minutes

Cook Time: 35 minutes

Servings: 6

Ingredients

1 diced large onion

1 tablespoon paprika

1 tablespoon minced garlic

1 1/2 pounds' lean ground beef

2 cups frozen sliced okra

3 cups fresh zucchini noodles

15 ounces can of drained whole kernel corn

28 ounces can tomato sauce

28 ounces can drained & diced tomatoes

salt & black pepper, to taste

shredded cheddar cheese toppings

Instructions

1. Using a large Dutch oven, add in the ground beef, olive oil and brown over medium high heat then drain the grease.

2. Add the garlic, onions and reduce the heat to a medium then cook until the veggies are translucent.

3. Add in the diced tomatoes. tomato sauce, pepper, salt, paprika, okra, zucchini and reduce the heat to a simmer for 20 minutes.

4. Serve and enjoy topped with the cheese.

Nutrition Information

Calories: 486kcal | Fat: 7.5g | Carbohydrates: 96.2g | Protein: 21.8g

Cheesy Red Pepper Dice

Preparation Time: 15 minutes

Cook Time: 20 minutes

Servings: 12

Ingredients

1/2 cup mayonnaise

1/2 teaspoon celery salt

1 teaspoon dijon mustard

1 teaspoon cayenne pepper

1 teaspoon smoked paprika

1 cup diced & roasted red peppers

2 cups grated cheddar cheese

2 cups grated sharp cheddar cheese

Instructions

1. Cut the red peppers open and remove all the seeds and stems then place face down on a parchment paper prepared sheet.

2. Transfer the sheet into the oven and bake for 20 minutes at 450°F until wrinkly and lightly charred then allow to cool off.

3. Peel the pepper skins off then dice into bits and set aside.

4. Combine the remaining ingredients together (except the salt) then add in the diced pepper and incorporate.

5. Season with the salt and taste to adjust, adding extra pepper if desired and enjoy.

Nutrition Information

Calories: 226kcal | Fat: 20.3g | Carbohydrates: 1.8g | Protein: 9.9g

Cheese Dip

Preparation Time: 15 minutes

Cook Time: 25 minutes

Servings: 5

Ingredients

3 diced green onions

8 ounces' cream cheese

11 ounces' pimento cheese

Instructions

1. Place the cream and pimento cheese into large mixing bowl and blend with an electric mixer.

2. Add the diced onions into the mix and blend again then scoop the mixture into a baking dish.

3. Bake the cheese onion mix until the edges are lightly browned for 20-25 minutes at 350°F.

4. Serve and enjoy with any side of your choice.

Nutrition Information

Calories: 358kcal | Fat: 28.8g | Carbohydrates: 20.3g | Protein: 5.1g

APPETIZER & SNACKS

Quick Muffin Cornbread

Preparation Time: 10 minutes

Cook Time: 15 minutes

Servings: 12

Ingredients

1/3 teaspoon salt

3/4 cup cheddar cheese, shredded

1 teaspoon baking powder

1 1/4 cups almond flour

3 large eggs

4 tablespoons melted butter

Instructions

1. Heat the oven up to 400°F then spray a 12 muffin pan with cooking oil spray and set aside.

2. Combine all the dry ingredients together then add in the wet ingredients and incorporate everything together.

3. Pour the dough into the muffin tins then bake in the heated oven until golden brown for 15 minutes.

4. Serve and enjoy or store for later consumption.

Nutrition Information

Calories: 224kcal | Fat: 20g | Carbohydrates: 3.6g | Protein: 8.7g

Simple Keto Biscuits

Preparation Time: 5 minutes

Cook Time: 12 minutes

Servings: 15

Ingredients

1/4 teaspoons salt

1/2 cup sour cream

1/2 cup shredded cheese

1/2 teaspoon powdered onion

1/2 teaspoon powdered garlic

1 tablespoon baking powder

1 1/2 cups almond flour

2 large eggs

4 tablespoons melted butter

Instructions

1. Heat the oven up to 450°F then incorporate all the ingredients together.

2. Spray a frying pan with cooking oil spray then drop dollops of the biscuit batter into the pan.

3. Place the pan into the oven and cook for 12 minutes.

4. Serve and enjoy as desired.

Nutrition Information

Calories: 164kcal | Fat: 14.6g | Carbohydrates: 4.6g | Protein: 5.9g

Classic Deviled Eggs

Preparation Time: 10 minutes

Cook Time: 0 minute

Servings: 7

Ingredients

1 tablespoon mustard

2 tablespoons sweet pickle relish

4 tablespoons mayonnaise

7 hard-boiled eggs

paprika, to sprinkle

salt & pepper, to taste

Instructions

1. Peel the boiled eggs and slice in half then scoop out the yolk into a mixing bowl.

2. Add the remaining ingredients into the mixing bowl then mash until blended and creamy.'

3. Scoop the creamy mixture into the egg whites then garnish with the paprika.

4. Serve and enjoy as desired.

Nutrition Information

Calories: 140kcal | Fat: 11.4g | Carbohydrates: 2.1g | Protein: 6.6g

Cheesy Zucchini Baked Fries

Preparation Time: 20 minutes

Cook Time: 30 minutes

Servings: 3

Ingredients

1 cup of mayonnaise

1 cup shredded parmesan cheese

3 medium zucchini

salt & pepper, to taste

Instructions

1. Using a small mixing bowl, add in the pepper, salt, parmesan cheese and stir together then set aside.

2. Horizontally halve the zucchini then slice each half into 4 even sticks.

3. Smear a thin layer of the mayonnaise on each cut side of the zucchini slices then run each slice through the cheese mixture.

4. Arrange the coated zucchini on a cooking oil sprayed baking sheet then bake for 20-30 minutes at 450°F.

5. Serve warm and enjoy as desired.

Nutrition Information

Calories: 647kcal | Fat: 64.2g | Carbohydrates: 6.4g| Protein: 10.7g

Ketogenic Sausage Balls

Preparation Time: 20 minutes

Cook Time: 20 minutes

Servings: 30

Ingredients

1/2 teaspoon salt

1 large egg

1 cup almond meal

1-pound breakfast sausage

1 cup sharp cheddar cheese

2 teaspoons baking powder

Instructions

1. Using a large mixing bowl, add in all the ingredients and combine using an electric mixer.

2. Scoop 30 balls from the mixture onto a slightly greased baking sheet.

3. Place the baking sheet in the oven and bake until slightly browned for 20 minutes at 350°F.

4. Serve and enjoy as desired.

Nutrition Information

Calories: 100kcal | Fat: 8.8g | Carbohydrates: 1g | Protein: 4.6g

No Bake Chocolate Cookies

Preparation Time: 15 minutes

Cook Time: 0 minute

Servings: 10

Ingredients

1/4 cup butter

1/4 cup heavy cream

1/2 cup swerve

1/2 cup chopped pecans

1/2 cup shredded coconut

1 teaspoon vanilla

2 tablespoons powdered cocoa

Instructions

1. Add the butter, cream & swerve into a pot, mix and boil for 2 minutes.

2. Take the pot off the heat then stir in the powdered cocoa, vanilla, pecans and coconut.

3. Scoop the butter out onto parchment papers then place in the refrigerator to harden.

4. Serve and enjoy as desired.

Nutrition Information

Calories: 273kcal | Fat: 22.9g | Carbohydrates: 25.6g | Protein: 3.2g

Simple Chocolate Mousse

Preparation Time: 5 minutes

Cook Time: 0 minute

Servings: 1

Ingredients

1/2 teaspoon vanilla

1 cup heavy cream

2 tablespoons sugar

3 tablespoons powdered cocoa

whipped cream, as desired

Instructions

1. Using a large mixing bowl, add in all the ingredients and combine together.

2. Using an immersion mixer, beat the mixture together until a stiff peak is formed and incorporated.

3. Refrigerate for an hour to set then serve and enjoy topped with whipped cream.

Nutrition Information

Calories: 936kcal | Fat: 82g | Carbohydrates: 41.3g | Protein: 3g

Delicious Ketogenic Berry Crisp

Preparation Time: 25 minutes

Cook Time: 30 minutes

Servings: 6

Ingredients

1 teaspoon swerve

3 cups strawberries

heavy cream, to taste

for the topping

1/2 cup melted butter

1/2 teaspoon cinnamon

1/2 cup pecans, chopped

1 teaspoon vanilla

1 1/2 cups almond meal

2 tablespoons swerve

Instructions

1. Using a large mixing bowl, add in the berries and sprinkle with the teaspoon of swerve and set aside.

2. Using a separate mixing bowl, add in the vanilla, cinnamon, melted butter, almond meal, swerve and mold together until a batter is formed.

3. Add in the pecans and stir until properly combined.

4. Pinch bits off the mixture and place over all the sweetened berries.

5. Bake the topped berries in the oven until slightly browned for 30 minutes at 350°F.

6. Serve and enjoy with heavy cream as desired.

Nutrition Information

Calories: 970kcal | Fat: 82.6g | Carbohydrates: 46.2g | Protein: 19.8g

Simple Tortillas Biscuit

Preparation Time: 10 minutes

Cook Time: 5 minutes

Servings: 10

Ingredients

1/4 teaspoon kosher salt

1 slightly beaten egg

1 teaspoon baking powder

2 teaspoons xanthan gum

2 teaspoons apple cider vinegar

3 teaspoons water

24g coconut flour

96g almond flour

Instructions

1. Add the coconut flour, almond flour, baking powder, xanthum gum and salt into a food processor then pulse until combined.

2. Pour the cider vinegar into the processor and process then add in the eggs and pulse to mix.

3. Add the spoons of water and mix until the dough is sticky to touch then mold into a ball shape.

4. Cover the dough with a cling film then knead for 2 minutes then allow to sit for 10 minutes.

5. Heat the skillet over medium heat, meanwhile break the dough into 10 even balls and roll each one out between parchment paper with a rolling pin.

6. Transfer the rolled out dough into the skillet at cook for 10 seconds then flip over and cook until slightly golden on both sides.

7. Serve immediately and enjoy as desired.

Nutrition Information

Calories: 89kcal | Fat: 6g | Carbohydrates: 4g | Protein: 3g

Simple Keto Buns Rolls

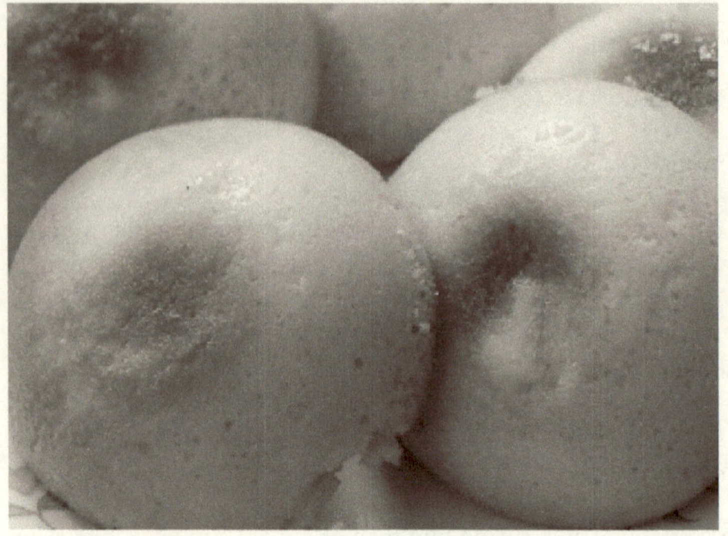

Preparation Time: 20 minutes

Cook Time: 40 minutes

Servings: 4

Ingredients

1/4 cup coconut flour

1/2 tablespoon apple cider vinegar

1 cup water

1 teaspoon baking powder

1 teaspoon dried thyme & oregano, if desired

2 egg yolks

2 tablespoons ground psyllium husks

4 egg whites

salt & pepper, to taste

Instructions

1. Heat the oven up to 350°F then prepare a baking sheet with parchment paper and set aside.

2. Whisk the egg whites together until a stiff peak forms then keep to the side.

3. Combine the remaining ingredients together in a separate bowl then carefully fold in the egg whites.

4. Mold out 4 evenly sized rolls from the dough then place on the baking sheet.

5. Place the baking sheet in the oven and bake until cooked through for 40 minutes.

6. Serve hot and enjoy.

Nutrition Information

Calories: 120kcal | Fat: 3.1g | Carbohydrates: 23.4g | Protein: 6g

Creamy Low Carb Oreos

Preparation Time: 15 minutes

Cook Time: 30 minutes

Servings: 10

Ingredients

for the cookies

1/4 cup powdered cacao

1/2 teaspoon baking soda

1 large egg

1 teaspoon vanilla extract

1 teaspoon apple cider vinegar

1 1/2 cups blanched almond meal

3 tablespoons olive oil

4 tablespoons erythritol

a pinch of salt

for the filling

1/2 cup of soaked cashews

1 teaspoon vanilla extract

2 tablespoons erythritol

3 tablespoons cacao butter

3 tablespoons melted butter

Instructions

1. Heat the oven up to 350°F then prepare a baking sheet with parchment paper.

2. Add all the cooking ingredients into a high speed blender the process until combined.

3. Roll the cookie mixture out until flat using a rolling pin then cut out 20 even round shaped from the dough.

4. Transfer the round shaped dough onto the baking sheet then bake for 15 minutes in the oven.

5. In the meantime, blend all the filling ingredients together until creamy and smooth then place in the fridge to become firm a bit.

6. Allow the cookies cool off then spoon a teaspoon of the creamy filling into the center of the cookie and spread around.

7. Top the cream filling with another cookie then place everything in the fridge until set.

8. Serve immediately and enjoy.

Nutrition Information

Calories: 269kcal | Fat: 25g | Carbohydrates: 13g | Protein: 6g

Ice Cream Cookie Sandwiches

Preparation Time: 13 minutes

Cook Time: 38 minutes

Servings: 4

Ingredients

for the cookie

1/3 cup chopped chocolate

1/2 teaspoon baking powder

1 large egg

1 teaspoon apple cider vinegar

2 teaspoons vanilla extract

2 cups blanched almond flour

3 tablespoons melted ghee

3 tablespoons collagen protein

a pinch of salt

stevia, to taste

for the cream

1/4 cup water

1/3 cup powdered cocoa

1 teaspoon juiced lime

1 teaspoon cinnamon, if desired

2 teaspoons vanilla extract

3 tablespoons melted coconut oil, with extra 2 teaspoons

3 1/2 tablespoons erythritol

3 1/2 tablespoons melted cacao butter

4 large eggs

5 egg yolks

6 tablespoons olive oil, with extra teaspoon

7 tablespoons melted ghee

Instructions

1. Heat the oven up to 340°F then line 2 baking sheets with parchment paper and set aside.

2. Use a small mixing bowl to combine the baking powder, salt, collagen protein and almond meal together.

3. Pour the cider vinegar in on top of the baking powder then add in the remaining ingredients and stir until combined then adjust the sweetness to taste.

4. Mold the mixture into balls then transfer onto the line baking sheets and press down until flat.

5. Place the sheets in the oven and bake until golden brown for 15 minutes then remove and allow to cool off.

6. Add all the cream ingredients into a high speed blender and blitz for 2 minutes.

7. Taste and adjust for sweetness then pour into an ice cream maker.

8. Churn the mixture for 20 minutes and transfer into a serving bowl then into the freezer to set for 20 minutes.

9. Top the cookies with a scoop of the ice cream then add another cookie piece on the cream and gently press down on it.

10. Repeat the same process until the cookies are exhausted then serve and enjoy.

Nutrition Information

Calories: 662kcal | Fat: 51g | Carbohydrates: 15g | Protein: 25g

Simple Ice Molds Pops

Preparation Time: 10 minutes

Cook Time: 4 minutes

Servings: 4

Ingredients

1 cup coconut cream

1 tablespoon cacao butter

1 teaspoon powdered vanilla

1 tablespoon unsweetened powdered chocolate 2 egg yolks

2 tablespoons collagelatin

2 tablespoon coconut oil

a pinch of salt

liquid stevia, to taste

Instructions

1. Using a small saucepan, add in the coconut oil, vanilla, coconut cream, salt, powdered chocolate, cacao butter, collagelatin and heat over low heat until melted and combined then take the pan off the heat.

2. Allow the mixture to cool off then pour into a high speed blender and add the egg yolks, stevia and blend until smooth and creamy.

3. Pour the mixture into ice molds then place in the freezer to set.

4. Top the pops with any topping of your choice and enjoy.

Nutrition Information

Calories: 303kcal | Fat: 26g | Carbohydrates: 6g | Protein: 11g

Enchilada Sauced Meatballs

Preparation Time: 5 minutes

Cook Time: 5 hours

Servings: 6

Ingredients

2 pounds frozen meatballs

28 ounces enchilada sauce

10 ounces drained rotel

1/2 cup shredded fiesta blend cheese

fresh diced cilantro, to garnish

Instructions

1. Using a crock post, add in the drained rotel, enchilada sauce, meat balls and set to cook for 4-5 hours on low settings or 3-4 hours on high settings.

2. Once done, add in the cheese atop and cover then allow to cook until the cheese melts for about 10 minutes.

3. Serve with a garnish of cilantro and enjoy.

Nutrition Information

Calories: 493kcal | Fat: 34g | Carbohydrate: 12g | Protein: 30g

Bun Mushroom Cheeseburgers

Preparation Time: 5 minutes

Cook Time: 15 minutes

Servings: 6

Ingredients

1-pound ground beef

1 teaspoon black pepper

1 tablespoon avocado oil

1 teaspoon pink Himalayan salt

1 tablespoon Worcestershire sauce

6 sharp cheddar cheese slices

6 rinsed & dry destemmed Portobello mushroom caps

Instructions

1. Use a mixing bowl to combine the Worcestershire sauce, ground beef, salt & pepper together.

2. Mold the beef into burger patties then use a big frying pan to heat avocado oil over medium heat.

3. Add in the Portobello mushroom caps and cook for 4 minutes per side then take off the heat.

4. Using the same pan, add in the burger patties and cook until a desired doneness is reached for 4 minutes per side.

5. Add the cheese atop the burgers then cover for a minute to allow the cheese to melt.

6. Layer one mushroom cap with the cheeseburger, any topping of your choice then cover with the remaining mushroom cap.

7. Serve and enjoy.

Nutrition Information

Calories: 336kcal | Fat: 22.8g | Carbohydrates: 4g | Protein: 29.1g

DESSERTS, CAKES & PIE RECIPES

Taco Chicken Pinwheels

Preparation Time: 10 minutes

Cook Time: 2 hours

Servings: 10

Ingredients

1/3 cup sour cream

1 teaspoon taco seasoning

1 cup shredded Colby jack cheese

2 tablespoons diced green chilies

7 flour tortilla wraps

8 ounces softened cream cheese

10 ounces' chicken, shredded

Instructions

1. Add the sour cream and cream cheese into a medium sized mixing bowl then whisk together with a hand mixer until smooth and creamy.

2. Add the cheese, taco seasoning, chicken and chilies into the mix then combine together.

3. Spread the mixture out onto each flour tortillas then roll up and seal.

4. Use a plastic wrap to wrap each of the sealed tortillas then place into the fridge for 1-2 hours.

5. Once chilled, remove the wrap from the tortillas and slice into pinwheels.

6. Serve and enjoy.

Nutrition Information

Calories: 255kcal | Fat: 16g | Carbohydrates: 12g | Protein: 13g

Pecan Vanilla Pie

Preparation Time: 25 minutes

Cook Time: 1 hour 5 minutes

Servings: 10 slices

Ingredients

for the crust

1/2 teaspoon pink himalayan salt

3/4 cup coconut flour

3/4 tablespoon olive oil

3/4 teaspoon vanilla extract

2 large eggs

3 tablespoons erythritol

6 tablespoon melted butter

for the filling

1 teaspoon vanilla extract

1 1/2 cups chopped raw pecans

2 large eggs

2 tablespoons melted butter

10 tablespoons erythritol

10 tablespoons maple syrup

Instructions

1. Add all the dry crust ingredients into a mixing bowl and combine together, do the same for the wet ingredients.

2. Combine the wet and dry ingredients mixture together and mold until a tender dough is formed.

3. Generously grease the dough all over then bake for 12 minutes at 350°F then set aside to cool off.

4. With a large mixing bowl, add in all the filling ingredient except the pecans and incorporate together.

5. Scatter the chopped pecans over the cooled crust then cover with the filling mixture.

6. Bake the pecan pie for 50 minutes at 350°F then allow to cool to taste.

7. Slice into 10 pieces, serve and enjoy.

Nutrition Information

Calories: 259.2kcal | Fat: 25g | Carbohydrates: 9.3g | Protein: 4.65g

Simple Butter Cake

Preparation Time: 10 minutes

Cook Time: 45 minutes

Servings: 16

Ingredients

1/4 cup egg white protein

1/2 teaspoon salt

1/2 cup heavy whipping cream

1 cup water

1 cup swerve

1 cup coconut flour

1 tablespoon baking powder

1 cup melted & salted butter

2 1/2 cups almond flour

3 teaspoons vanilla extract

7 large eggs

Instructions

1. Using a mixer, incorporate the swerve and melted butter together until combined.

2. Pour in the dry ingredients into the butter mixture and incorporate.

3. Add in the wet ingredients and mix everything together until thick.

4. Coat a frying pan with cooking oil spray then sprinkle with the coconut flour.

5. Transfer the mixture into the flour prepared pan and bake until golden brown for 40-50 minutes at 350°F.

6. Top with cream cheese frosting and enjoy as desired.

Nutrition Information

Calories: 267kcal | Fat: 25g | Carbohydrates: 7.1g | Protein: 8.2g

Mayo Deviled Eggs

Preparation Time: 15 minutes

Cook Time: 15 minutes

Servings: 12

Ingredients

1/8 teaspoon pepper

1/4 teaspoon salt

1/2 teaspoon dry mustard

5 Tablespoons mayonnaise

6 boiled eggs

handful of paprika

Instructions

1. Vertically half the boiled eggs then scoop the yolks out and smash with a folk.

2. Combine the smashed yolk with the pepper, dry mustard and salt.

3. Pour in the mayo and incorporate until a desired consistency is achieved.

4. Fill the whites with the mayo yolk mixture.

5. Serve with a garnish of paprika and enjoy.

Nutrition Information

Calories: 79kcal | Fat: 7g | Carbohydrates: 0.5g | Protein: 3.2g

Fried Okra Slices

Preparation Time: 5 minutes

Cook Time: 5 minutes

Servings: 5

Ingredients

1/4 teaspoon salt

1/4 teaspoon pepper

1/3 cup almond flour

1/2 tablespoon coconut oil

1-pound fresh okra

Instructions

1. Slice the okra into 1/4" slices then discard the stems.

2. Add the coconut oil into a large skillet and heat over medium high heat.

3. Using a medium mixing bowl, add in the almond flour, pepper, salt, okra slices and incorporate together.

4. Transfer the okra into the hot oil then stir together until browned and tenderized.

5. Drain the oil from the okra, serve and enjoy as desired.

Nutrition Information

Calories: 130kcal | Fat: 10g | Carbohydrates: 7g | Protein: 3g

Cheese Stuffed Chicken

Preparation Time: 20 minutes

Cook Time: 28 minutes

Servings: 4

Ingredients

1/4 teaspoon salt

1/2 cup marinara sauce

1/2 teaspoon powdered garlic

3/4 cup ricotta cheese

1 full teaspoon Italian seasoning

1 cup divided shredded mozzarella cheese

2 skinless & boneless chicken breasts

3 tablespoons avocado oil

salt & pepper, to taste

Instructions

1. Using a medium mixing bowl, add in 1/2 cup of mozzarella cheese, Italian seasoning, ricotta cheese, salt and stir together until incorporated.

2. Place the chicken breast on chopping boards then gently create a pocket into the chicken.

3. Using a large skillet add in 2 tablespoons oil then heat over medium high heat.

4. Fill the chicken pockets with cheese mixture then sprinkle with the salt, pepper, powdered garlic and lower into the heated skillet and cook for 5 minutes then flip over and cook for an extra 5 minutes.

5. Take the skillet off the heat then top with the marinara sauce, sprinkle with the remaining mozzarella cheese and bake in the oven until cooked through for 10-15 minutes at 450°F.

6. Serve and enjoy.

Calories: 851kcal | Fat: 32.4g | Carbohydrates: 6.4g | Protein: 132.2g

Coconut Chocolate Cauliflower Meal

Preparation Time: 15 minutes

Cook Time: 20 minutes

Servings: 4

Ingredients

1/4 teaspoon salt

1 collagen scoop

1 scoop mito sweet

1 cauliflower head

1 tablespoon stevia

1 tablespoon coconut oil

1 cup full-fat coconut milk

1 1/2 tablespoons powdered cacao

4 beaten large eggs

cacao nibs, if desired

Instructions

1. Chop the cauliflower head into florets then heat a medium saucepan over medium heat.

2. Add the coconut milk into the saucepan and bring to a simmer then add in the cauliflower florets and stir until combined.

3. Reduce the heat to a low then allow the cauliflower to continue cooking for 4 minutes until thickened.

4. Add the beaten eggs into the pan and fold in along with the salt, stevia, mito sweet, powdered cocoa and collagen powder.

5. Allow the eggs to cook through and thicken while stirring continually.

6. Serve and enjoy garnished with the cocoa nibs.

Nutrition Information

Calories: 464.9kcal | Fat: 41.2g | Carbohydrates: 18g | Protein: 22.1g

ChocoLava Cake

Preparation Time: 7 minutes

Cook Time: 13 minutes

Servings: 2

Ingredients

1/8 cup chocolate chunks

1/8 teaspoon kosher salt

1 tablespoon erythritol

1 tablespoon almond flour

1 teaspoon vanilla extract

2 large eggs

2 ounces' chocolate

2 ounces' ghee, with extra

2 tablespoons powdered erythritol

handful of fresh berries, to serve

Instructions

1. Heat the oven up to 350°F then generously coat 2 ramekins with the extra ghee.

2. With a small saucepan, add in the 2 ounces of ghee, chocolate and melt together over low heat then set aside.

3. Use an hand mixer to beat the vanilla, eggs and salt together until frothy

4. Combine the vanilla and chocolate mixture together then add in the erythritol, almond flour and mix to blend.

5. Fill the coated ramekins up to half with the batter top with the chocolate chunks and fill up with the remaining batter.

6. Bake until the tops are set for 9 minutes, sprinkle with the powdered erythtitol then allow to cool off.

7. Serve and enjoy topped with the fresh berries.

Nutrition Information

Calories: 559kcal | Fat: 52g | Carbohydrates: 27.9g | Protein: 9.7g

Bacon & Mayo Deviled Eggs

Preparation Time: 20 minutes

Cook Time: 10 minutes

Servings: 12

Ingredients

1/4 cup mayonnaise

1 tablespoon dry parsley flakes

2 chopped & seeded cherry tomatoes

3 cooked & crumbled bacon slices, with extra for garnish

6 boiled large eggs

salt & black pepper, to taste

Instructions

1. Vertically halve the eggs then remove the yolks and place inside a medium mixing bowl.

2. Smash the yolks then add in the parsley, tomatoes, bacon, mayonnaise and stir together.

3. Add in the salt, pepper and blend together until combined.

4. Fill the egg whites with the yolk mixture then top with the crumbled bacon.

5. Serve and enjoy as desired.

Grilled Artichokes with Cream Dip

Preparation Time: 30 minutes

Cook Time: 35 minutes

Servings: 6

Ingredients

1/4 cup sour cream

1 cup mayonnaise

1 1/2 tablespoons chopped fresh rosemary

2 halved limes

4 bacon strips

6 medium fresh artichokes

8 cups water

Instructions

1. Trim the artichokes and set aside then boil the water and halved limes using a Dutch oven over medium high heat.

2. Add three artichokes into the boiling water and boil for 7 minutes then drain and repeat the same process for the remaining artichoke.

3. Allow the artichokes to cool off then vertically slice, dispose the fuzzy choke from each half and set aside.

4. With a small skillet, add in the bacon slices and cook until crispy then crumble, reserving a tablespoon of the dripping.

5. Combine the sour cream, rosemary, mayonnaise, bacon drippings, crumbled bacon and place inside the refrigerator.

6. Coat a cooking grill with cooking oil spray then heat up to a medium high heat.

7. Arrange the cut side of the artichokes down on the grill and grill for 5 minutes per side until tenderized.

8. Serve and enjoy with the dip and a topping of rosemary.

Nutrition Information

Calories: 294kcal | Fat: 30.6g | Carbohydrates: 3.3g | Protein: 1.3g

Creamy Pecan Pie

Preparation Time: 30 minutes

Cook Time: 1 hour 10 minutes

Servings: 10 slices

Ingredients

for the crust

1 sweet pie crust

for the filling

1/2 cup erythritol

1/2 teaspoon pink salt

3/4 cup unsalted butter

1 large egg

1 1/2 cups chopped raw pecans

1 1/2 teaspoon beef gelatin powder

1 3/4 cup heavy whipping cream

15 drops liquid stevia

Instructions

1. Bake the pie crust for 10 minutes at 350°F then set aside to cool off.

2. Using a large saucepan, pour in the erythritol, butter and melt cook for 7 minutes over medium low heat.

3. Carefully add in the heavy cream, reserving a 1/4 cup aside and bring to a simmer until thickened for 15-20 minutes.

4. Take the pan off the heat then add in the stevia, vanilla extract and stir together then set aside to cool.

5. Combine the gelatin with the remaining heavy cream and incorporate then whisk the large egg in a separate bowl.

6. Drizzle 1/4 cup of the heated cream mixture into the whisked egg then gently add in the remaining mixture and gelatin mix.

7. Layer the cooled crust with the chopped pecans then pour on the cream mixture, cover the crust edges with foil and bake until set for 50 minutes.

8. Allow the pie to cool off then slice into 10, serve and enjoy.

Nutrition Information

Calories: 505kcal | Fat: 51g | Carbohydrates: 7g | Protein: 7g

Hot Savannah CrabMeat Dip

Preparation Time: 20 minutes

Cook Time: 40 minutes

Servings: 4

Ingredients

1/4 cup diced green onions

1/4 cup grated Parmesan cheese

1/2 teaspoon dry mustard

3/4 cup mayonnaise

1-pound crabmeat

1 teaspoon hot sauce

1 cup grated pepper jack cheese

2 tablespoons juice lime

3 tablespoons Worcestershire sauce

6 minced garlic cloves

salt & pepper, to taste

Instructions

1. Heat the oven up to 325°F then toss the jack cheese and crab meat together in a large mixing bowl.

2. Add the mayonnaise, pepper, hot sauce, mustard, salt, garlic, lime, green onions, Worcestershire sauce, parmesan cheese and incorporate together until combined.

3. Transfer the mixture onto a greased baking pan then bake for 40 minutes.

4. Serve and enjoy with tortillas, biscuits or toast.

Nutrition Information

Calories: 504kcal | Fat: 43.1g | Carbohydrates: 6.8g | Protein: 32.4g

Roasted Okra Slices

Preparation Time: 5 minutes

Cook Time: 10 minutes

Servings: 3

Ingredients

1 tablespoon avocado oil

18 sliced & trimmed fresh okra pods

salt & black pepper, to taste

Instructions

1. Heat the oven up to 425°F then prepare a baking sheet with aluminum foil.

2. Arrange the okra on the baking sheet in a single layer then drizzle with the oil, salt & pepper.

3. Place the baking sheet in the oven and bake for 10-15 minutes until golden and crispy at the edges.

4. Serve and enjoy as desired.

Nutrition Information

Calories: 438kcal | Fat: 6.6g | Carbohydrates: 77.7g | Protein: 28.4g

Fried Green Tomato Slices

Preparation Time: 10 minutes

Cook Time: 10 minutes

Servings: 4

Ingredients

1/4 cup bacon fat

1/4 teaspoon cayenne pepper

1/2 teaspoon powdered garlic

1 large egg

1 cup almond flour

1 teaspoon powdered onion

2 tablespoons water

2 medium green tomatoes

sea salt & black pepper, to taste

Instructions

1. Slice the tomatoes into 1/4" thickness then season with the salt and allow to sit for 5 minutes.

2. Using a small mixing bowl, add in the egg and whisk with water.

3. Get another mixing bowl and add in the pepper, salt, cayenne powder, powdered garlic & onion, almond flour and combine together.

4. Heat the bacon fat up in a large skillet over medium high heat.

5. Meanwhile, dip the tomato slices in the egg then run through the flour mix, shaking off any excesses.

6. Fry the tomato slices until golden brown for 3-5 minutes per side.

7. Transfer onto a paper towel to drain then season with salt again if desired, serve and enjoy.

Nutrition Information

Calories: 203kcal | Fat: 17.9g | Carbohydrates: 8g | Protein: 4.3g

END

Thank you for reading my book.

Diane Brown